Similarities and differences: A comparison of current UK GAAP, new UK GAAP (FRS 102) and IFRS

UK Accounting Consulting Services
PricewaterhouseCoopers LLP, Chartered Accountants

Published by

Bloomsbury Professional

Bloomsbury Professional, an imprint of Bloomsbury Publishing Plc, Maxwelton House, 41–43 Boltro Road, Haywards Heath, West Sussex, RH16 1BJ

ISBN 9781780438313

British Library Cataloguing-in-Publication Data.
A catalogue record for this book is available from the British Library.

Printed in Great Britain.
Typeset by YHT Ltd, 4 Hercies Road, Hillingdon, Middlesex UB10 9NA

Similarities and differences: A comparison of current UK GAAP, new UK GAAP (FRS 102) and IFRS

Contents

Introduction

This publication provides a high-level overview of the significant differences between 'old' UK GAAP, new UK GAAP (which, for the purposes of this publication, means FRS 102, 'The financial reporting standard applicable in the UK and Republic of Ireland') and EU-adopted IFRS ('IFRS'). It focuses on a selection of those differences most commonly found in practice.

'Old UK GAAP' refers to the SSAPs, FRSs and UITF Abstracts in existence at March 2013, when FRS 102 was issued, which are superseded by FRS 102 when it is applicable.

'New UK GAAP' refers to the version of FRS 102 applicable for accounting periods beginning on or after 1 January 2015. This comprises the original version issued in March 2013, together with amendments for:

- Basic financial instruments and hedge accounting (issued July 2014).
- Pension obligations (issued February 2015).
- Share-based payment transactions with cash alternatives (included in the amendments issued in July 2015).

In addition, this publication includes details of the amendments issued by the Financial Reporting Council (FRC) in July 2015, to ensure consistency with the changes in company law resulting from the EU Accounting Directive, that apply for accounting periods beginning on or after 1 January 2016.

When applying the individual accounting frameworks, companies should consult all of the relevant accounting standards and, where applicable, the relevant legislation.

Where this publication states 'Same as old UK GAAP' or 'Same as IFRS', this means that the guidance is identical to old UK GAAP or IFRS, although the standards might use different terminology or wording. Where it states 'Similar', this means that the guidance is not identical and there are minor differences.

Qualifying entities applying the recognition and measurement rules of IFRS may be exempt from certain disclosures if they apply the reduced disclosure framework in FRS 101, 'Reduced disclosure framework'. In this case, there are some changes that are required to the IASB's texts in order to ensure compliance with the Companies Act 2006. Where such a change is applicable, details are included in the relevant sections in the IFRS column below. There are equivalent disclosure exemptions in FRS 102.

Abbreviations used include:

- FRS application guidance – the FRC's new framework, FRS 100, 'Application of financial reporting requirements';
- New UK GAAP – for the purposes of this publication, this means FRS 102, 'The financial reporting standard applicable in the UK and Republic of Ireland', which is based on the IFRS for SMEs but amended to permit some previous accounting treatments in old UK GAAP and to comply with the Companies Act 2006; and
- RDF (IFRS) – EU-adopted IFRS as amended to comply with the Companies Act 2006 and reduced-disclosure framework, available for qualifying subsidiaries and parents as set out in FRS 101, 'Reduced disclosure framework'.

While every effort has been made to ensure accuracy, information contained in this publication may not be comprehensive or information may have been omitted that may be relevant to a particular reader. In particular, this publication is not intended as a study of all aspects of old UK GAAP, new UK GAAP or IFRS, or as a substitute for reading the standards and interpretations when dealing with specific issues. No responsibility for loss to any person acting or refraining from acting as a result of any material in this publication can be accepted by PricewaterhouseCoopers. Readers should not act on the basis of this publication without seeking professional advice.

Executive summary

This executive summary has the following aims: to demonstrate how converting to new UK GAAP or IFRS has implications far beyond an entity's financial reporting function; to highlight some of the key differences between old UK GAAP, new UK GAAP and IFRS; and to encourage early consideration of the most appropriate framework to adopt in future for an entity.

This summary takes into account authoritative pronouncements issued under UK GAAP to July 2015 and amendments to *EU adopted* IFRS that are effective for years ending 31 December 2015. The requirements specific to banking companies, insurance companies and limited liability partnerships are outside the scope of this publication.

This publication does not cover in detail the requirements in FRS 102 applicable to small entities (that have replaced the 'Financial reporting standard for smaller entities (FRSSE)) or the requirements in FRS 105, 'The financial reporting standard applicable to the micro-entities regime'.

This publication also includes details of the amendments to new UK GAAP issued by the FRC in July 2015, to ensure compliance with the new Companies, Partnerships, and Groups (Accounts and Reports) Regulations 2015 (SI 2015/980). The most significant changes impact smaller companies, but there are other changes that might be relevant to any entity reporting under new UK GAAP. Most of these amendments are effective for accounting periods beginning on or after 1 January 2016, with early adoption permitted provided that changes to company law are implemented at the same time.

If there are future changes to the standards, we will continue to update the electronic version of this publication. This 'Executive summary' and the 'Summary of the key differences' will be published electronically and will be freely available on Inform at inform.pwc.com or by scanning the QR codes below.

Executive summary

Summary of key differences

Accounting areas with significant differences are outlined below.

Financial statements	**Old UK GAAP:** The following are required: (a) balance sheet, (b) profit and loss account, (c) statement of total recognised gain and losses, (d) cash flow statement (unless exempt), and (e) notes comprising a summary of the accounting policies, estimations and additional information. **New UK GAAP (FRS 102):** The same primary statements as under IFRS are required to be presented (with some exemptions for cash flow statements). If the only changes to equity during the period are a result of profit or loss, payment of dividends, correction of prior-period material errors or changes in accounting policy, a combined statement of income and retained earnings can be presented instead of both a statement of comprehensive income and a statement of changes in equity. The formats for the income statement and balance sheet are based on company law, but as a result of changes to the law arising from the implementation of the EU Accounting Directive, entities have the option to adapt the Companies Act formats subject to minimum disclosure requirements in FRS 102. The change to the formats applies for accounting periods beginning on or after 1 January 2016. If the entity elects to early adopt the change in formats, as permitted by law, it must also adopt the July 2015 amendments to FRS 102 in full. **IFRS:** Requires (a) statement of financial position, (b) statement of comprehensive income (presented as either a single statement or an income statement followed by a statement of other comprehensive income), (c) cash flow statement, (d) statement of changes in equity (presenting a reconciliation of equity items between the beginning and end of the period), and (e) notes.
Cash flow statement	**Old UK GAAP:** This requires the movement of cash (defined as cash in hand and deposits repayable on demand, less overdrafts) to be reported in the cash flow statement. There is no concept of 'cash equivalents'. Cash flows are reported in greater detail (under nine standard headings) than under new UK GAAP and IFRS. **New UK GAAP (FRS 102):** The presentation of the cash flow statement is similar to that under IFRS, showing movements on cash and cash equivalents, and with fewer standard headings than under old UK GAAP. New UK GAAP includes some exemptions from preparing cash flow statements, similar to old UK GAAP. **IFRS:** The presentation of the cash flow statement differs substantially from the presentation under old UK GAAP. The cash flows reported under IFRS relate to movements in cash and cash equivalents (defined as short-term highly liquid investments that are readily convertible into known amounts of cash and subject to insignificant risk of changes in value). IFRS has none of the exemptions that allow many entities not to prepare cash flow statements under UK GAAP (old and new).
Financial instruments	**Old UK GAAP:** All entities must apply FRS 25's presentation requirements (based on IAS 32) and company law disclosure requirements. Entities then determine which model they should apply: the 'old pre-FRS 26 UK GAAP' model (FRS 4, FRS 13 and, voluntarily, FRS 29) or the 'FRS 26' model (FRS 26 and FRS 29). This will depend on the entity's status, in particular its listing status, and whether it follows the company law fair value accounting rules. FRS 26 is based on IAS 39, which distinguishes four measurement categories of financial assets. These are: • financial assets at fair value through profit or loss; • held-to-maturity investments (measured at amortised costs); • loans and receivables (measured at amortised costs); and • available-for-sale financial assets (measured at fair value). For entities not applying FRS 26, financial instruments are carried at amortised cost.

	New UK GAAP (FRS 102): There are two sections dealing with financial instruments: section 11 addresses simple payables and receivables, and other basic financial instruments; and section 12 addresses other, more complex financial instruments. Most basic financial instruments are measured at amortised cost; complex instruments are generally measured at fair value through profit or loss. Alternatively, instead of sections 11 and 12, entities may apply the recognition and measurement requirements of IAS 39, or the recognition and measurement requirements of IFRS 9. The impairment model in FRS 102 is based on the principles in IAS 39 and the hedging model in IFRS 9. **IFRS (IAS 32 and 39):** Same as old UK GAAP for FRS 26 reporters, because FRS 26 is based on IAS 39. All entities must apply IAS 32 and IAS 39. IAS 39 is to be replaced by IFRS 9 which contains new rules on the classification and measurement of financial assets and financial liabilities, impairment and hedging. IFRS 9 is effective from 1 January 2018. New guidance on macro hedge accounting has not yet been finalised.
Expense recognition	**Old UK GAAP:** Research costs are expensed as incurred; development costs may be capitalised and amortised if specific criteria are met (as an accounting policy choice). Borrowing costs are capitalised if certain criteria are met. **New UK GAAP (FRS 102):** Similar to old UK GAAP, all research costs are recognised as an expense. Capitalisation is an accounting policy choice for development costs and for borrowing costs if certain criteria are met. **IFRS:** Similar to old UK GAAP, except that capitalisation of development costs is mandatory where the criteria for capitalisation are met.
Retirement benefits – defined benefit plans	**Old UK GAAP:** FRS 17 deals only with retirement benefits, and does not specifically address other employee benefits. Defined benefit plan liabilities are measured on an actuarial basis, using the projected unit credit method. Plan assets are measured at fair value. For the income statement, expected returns on plan assets are calculated separately from interest costs on the plan liabilities using different interest rates. Actuarial gains and losses are recognised in the statement of total recognised gains and losses in the period they arise. There is an exemption for group defined benefit plans such that, in certain circumstances, all entities in the group for their stand alone accounts can treat their participation in the plan as if it were a defined contribution plan. **New UK GAAP (FRS 102):** FRS 102's scope is wider than old UK GAAP. All employee benefits (except share-based payments) are in scope. For calculating defined benefit plan liabilities, the projected unit credit method is required. Plan assets are measured at fair value. The calculation of net interest costs under FRS 102 differs from old UK GAAP. Net interest cost is calculated by applying a single discount rate to the net defined benefit liability or asset. Remeasurements of the net defined benefit liability (that is, actuarial gains and losses) are recognised in full immediately in other comprehensive income. The accounting for group defined benefit plans differs from old UK GAAP: the cost of a defined benefit plan is recognised in the financial statements of the group entity that is legally the sponsoring employer for the plan if the net defined benefit costs are not allocated to other entities in the group. **IFRS:** The scope of IAS 19 is the same as FRS 102. The projected unit credit method is required for calculating defined benefit liabilities. Plan assets are measured at fair value. Under IAS 19, remeasurements, for example actuarial gains or losses, are recognised immediately in other comprehensive income. IAS 19 is also similar to new UK GAAP in the method of calculating net interest on the net defined benefit liability or

	asset. For group defined benefit plans, the net defined benefit cost is recognised in the financial statements of the group entity that is legally the sponsoring employer for the plan if the net defined benefit costs are not allocated to other entities in the group.
Deferred tax	**Old UK GAAP:** Deferred tax is recognised based on timing differences (with certain exceptions) using an incremental liability approach – timing differences are differences between an entity's taxable profits and its results as stated in the financial statements. This is a fundamentally different approach from IFRS. Deferred tax assets are recognised to the extent that they are recoverable (that is, it is more likely than not that there will be suitable taxable profits from which the future reversal of timing differences can be deducted). **New UK GAAP (FRS 102):** Deferred tax is recognised based on timing differences, with additional recognition requirements for certain other differences (a 'timing differences plus' approach). This approach requires the recognition of deferred tax for timing differences on the revaluation of assets and on assets (except goodwill) and liabilities arising on a business combination. In many cases, the resulting deferred tax will be similar to the temporary difference approach under IFRS. The criteria for recognising deferred tax assets are similar to old UK GAAP and IFRS. **IFRS:** Deferred tax is recognised on the basis of temporary differences. Temporary differences are differences between the carrying amount of an asset or liability in the financial statements and its tax base (that is, the amount that the entity expects will affect the taxable profit when the carrying amount of the asset or liability is recovered or settled). No deferred tax is recognised where a temporary difference arises on the initial recognition of an asset and liability in a transaction that is not a business combination and affects neither accounting profit nor taxable profit at the time of the transaction. The criteria for recognising deferred tax assets are similar to old and new UK GAAP.
Tangible and intangible fixed assets	**Old UK GAAP:** A cost or valuation model may be used for tangible fixed assets. Similarly, a cost or valuation model may be used for intangible assets; but a valuation model may only be used where an intangible asset has a readily ascertainable market value. There is a rebuttable presumption that goodwill and intangible assets have a useful economic life of 20 years. Goodwill with an indefinite life is not amortised. Any negative goodwill is recognised in profit or loss in the periods in which the non-monetary assets are recovered, with any excess recognised over the period expected to benefit. Goodwill and other intangibles with useful lives of more than 20 years are tested annually for impairment. Non-financial assets are tested for impairment only where there is an indication of impairment. All impairment losses (including on goodwill) may be reversed in future periods if relevant criteria are met. **New UK GAAP (FRS 102):** A cost or valuation model may be used for tangible and intangible fixed assets. All intangible assets, including goodwill, are assumed to have finite lives and are amortised. If the entity is unable to make a reliable estimate, the useful life is five years (but this is changed to 10 years in the July 2015 amendments to FRS 102). It is expected that entities transitioning from old UK GAAP to FRS 102 will maintain their existing life for definite-lived intangible assets and goodwill. Non-financial assets are tested for impairment only where there is an indication of impairment. Negative goodwill is recognised in profit or loss in the periods in which the non-monetary assets are recovered, with any excess recognised over the period expected to benefit. Impairment losses for goodwill should not be reversed in subsequent periods (under the July 2015 amendments to FRS 102). **IFRS:** For tangible and intangible assets, there is an accounting policy choice between the cost model and the revaluation (fair value) model. Goodwill and other intangibles with indefinite lives are reviewed annually for impairment and are not amortised. Non-financial assets with definite lives are amortised and tested for impairment only where there is an indication of impairment. Negative goodwill is recognised immediately. Impairment losses on goodwill are not reversed.

	UK entities reporting under FRS 101 RDF (IFRS) must consider whether non-amortisation of goodwill is an appropriate true and fair override of the Companies Act 2006. The same will apply for indefinite-lived intangible assets when SI 2015/980 applies. Any negative goodwill is recognised in profit or loss in the periods in which the non-monetary assets are recovered, with any excess recognised over the period expected to benefit.
Investment properties	**Old UK GAAP:** Investment properties are included in the balance sheet at open market value (through the statement of total recognised gains and losses). The cost model is not permitted. **New UK GAAP (FRS 102):** Investment property is carried at fair value (through profit or loss) if this fair value can be measured without undue cost or effort; otherwise, it is carried at cost within 'Property, plant and equipment'. **IFRS:** IAS 40, 'Investment property', offers a choice between fair value (through profit or loss) and the cost method.
Assets held for sale	**Old UK GAAP and new UK GAAP (FRS 102):** Assets held for sale are not covered; the decision to sell an asset is considered an impairment indicator. **IFRS:** IFRS 5, 'Non-current assets held for sale and discontinued operations', requires non-current assets to be classified as held for sale where the carrying amount is recovered principally through a sale transaction rather than through continuing use.
Business combinations	**Old UK GAAP:** Directly attributable transaction costs are included in the cost of acquisition. The cost of acquisition should include a reasonable estimate of the present value of contingent consideration expected to be paid in the future. The cost of acquisition is adjusted when revised estimates of amounts expected to be paid in the future are made. In some circumstances, merger accounting is applied. **New UK GAAP (FRS 102):** Similar to old UK GAAP. Transaction costs are included in the cost of acquisition. Contingent consideration is included as part of the acquisition cost if it is probable that the amount will be paid and it can be measured reliably. The cost of the acquisition is adjusted when revised estimates of amounts expected to be paid in the future are made. In some circumstances, merger accounting may be applied. **IFRS:** Transaction costs are expensed. Contingent consideration is recognised, regardless of the probability of payment. Contingent consideration that is classified as an equity instrument is not remeasured. Changes in contingent consideration that is classified as a financial liability are recognised in profit or loss.
Investments in associates and joint ventures	**Old UK GAAP:** Investments in associates are generally accounted for using the equity method in consolidated financial statements. Investments in joint ventures are accounted for using the 'gross equity' method, which is a form of equity accounting with additional disclosures in the profit and loss account and balance sheet. Investments in associates and joint ventures apply the cost model or fair value in separate financial statements. **New UK GAAP (FRS 102):** Investments in associates are generally accounted for using the equity method in consolidated financial statements. An investor that is not a parent can account for all of its investments in associates using either the cost model or the fair value model (with gains recognised either through other comprehensive income or through profit or loss). **IFRS:** Investments in associates and joint ventures are accounted for using the equity method. The cost and fair value models are generally not permitted.

Summary of key differences

Summary of key differences between old UK GAAP, new UK GAAP (FRS 102) and IFRS

The summary below highlights the key differences between old UK GAAP, new UK GAAP (that is, FRS 102) and IFRS.

The summary reflects the amendments to FRS 102 published in July 2015.

Key:

1	Same or minor differences
2	Some differences
3	Significant differences

Subject	Old UK GAAP vs New UK GAAP (FRS 102)		Old UK GAAP vs IFRS		IFRS vs New UK GAAP (FRS 102)	
Financial statements presentation	2	Company law formats apply for both, but a change in law and an amendment to FRS 102 means formats based on IFRS can be used under new UK GAAP.	2	Companies Act formats differ from IAS 1 formats.	2	IAS 1 formats differ from detailed company law formats used in FRS 102 (but under the amended FRS 102, there is also an option to use formats based on IFRS).
Cash flow statements	3	Cash vs Cash and cash equivalents. Also, FRS 102 has fewer headings.	3	Cash vs Cash and cash equivalents. Also, IFRS has fewer headings.	1	Both prepared for cash and cash equivalents. Similar headings.
Financial assets and liabilities: – FRS 4 model	3	Fair values (for example, for derivatives) not used under FRS 4.	3	Fair values not used under FRS 4. IAS 39 has detailed rules.	n/a	
– FRS 26/IAS 39 model	2	Measurement of financial assets may differ as no fair value through 'OCI' category under new UK GAAP. Also, different rules for hedge accounting.	1	FRS 26 is based on IAS 39.	2	Measurement of financial assets may differ as no fair value through 'OCI' category under new UK GAAP. Also, different rules for hedge accounting.
Foreign currency (SSAP 20)	2	Contracted rates can be used under SSAP 20. More flexible hedging of investments in entity accounts under SSAP 20	2	Contracted rates can be used under SSAP 20. More flexible hedging of investments in entity accounts under SSAP 20. CTA recycling under IFRS.	n/a	
Foreign currency (FRS 23)	2	No recycling of CTA under new UK GAAP.	1	FRS 23 is based on IAS 21.	2	No recycling of CTA under new UK GAAP
Hyperinflation	1		1	FRS 24 is based on IAS 29. UITF 9 permitted a choice of methods.	1	
Revenue recognition	1		1		1	
Government grants	2	Policy choice (accruals/ performance model) under FRS 102. Old UK GAAP uses accruals model.	1	Both use the accruals model.	2	Policy choice (accruals/performance model) under FRS 102. IFRS uses accrual model.
Capitalisation of borrowing costs	2	Policy choice under FRS 102.	1	Capitalisation required under both.	2	Policy choice under FRS 102.

Subject	Old UK GAAP vs New UK GAAP (FRS 102)		Old UK GAAP vs IFRS		IFRS vs New UK GAAP (FRS 102)	
Retirement benefits	2	Net interest cost approach and group schemes differ.	2	Net interest cost approach and group schemes differ.	1	FRS 102 is similar to IAS 19.
Other employee benefits	3	No standard under old UK GAAP.	3	No standard under old UK GAAP.	1	FRS 102 is similar to IAS 19.
Share-based payment transactions	2	Option pricing models not always applied under FRS 102. Also, arrangements where the counterparty has a choice of settlement are treated differently.	1	FRS 20 is based on IFRS 2.	2	Option pricing models not always applied under FRS 102. Also, arrangements where the counterparty has a choice of settlement are treated differently.
Income taxes – Current	1		1		1	
– Deferred	3	More deferred tax under FRS 102 'timing differences plus' approach. Unlike old GAAP there are no exceptions for revaluations, rollover and unremitted earnings A temporary difference approach is applied for business combinations.	3	Timing difference with exceptions vs temporary difference approaches.	2	Timing difference 'plus' vs temporary difference approaches although in many cases the resulting deferred tax from the different approaches will be the same.
Intangible assets other than goodwill	2	More intangibles under FRS 102 and no indefinite life.	2	More intangibles under IFRS.	2	IFRS can have indefinite-lived intangibles.
Property, plant and equipment	1		1		1	
Investment property	2	Fair value movement in statement of total recognised gains and losses (old UK GAAP) vs profit or loss (FRS 102).	2	Fair value movement in statement of total recognised gains and losses (old UK GAAP) vs profit or loss (IFRS).	1	Fair value movement in profit or loss for both.
Impairment of non-financial assets	2	Annual impairment testing required for some goodwill and intangibles under old UK GAAP. Reversals of goodwill impairments will be prohibited under FRS 102.	2	Allocation and reversal of impairment losses differ.	1	Same, when the July 2015 amendment to FRS 101 prohibiting reversal of impairment of goodwill applies.
Leases	2	Guidance more detailed in old UK GAAP. No 90% test in FRS 102.	2	Different methods for lessor accounting. Guidance more detailed in old UK GAAP. No 90% test in IFRS.	1	

Key:

1	Same or minor differences
2	Some differences
3	Significant differences

Subject	Old UK GAAP vs New UK GAAP (FRS 102)		Old UK GAAP vs IFRS		IFRS vs New UK GAAP (FRS 102)	
Inventories	1		1		1	
Provisions and contingencies	1		1		1	
Events after the reporting period	1		1	FRS 21 is based on IAS 10.	1	
Consolidation	2	Subsidiaries held in investment portfolios are not consolidated under FRS 102.	2	No remeasurement of pre-existing or retained stakes under old UK GAAP. Investment entities are not consolidated under IFRS.	2	No remeasurement of pre-existing or retained stakes under FRS 102.
Business combinations (including goodwill)	2	Goodwill has to be amortised under FRS 102. Useful life is no longer 'presumed' to be 20 years (as it was under old UK GAAP).	2	Goodwill is not amortised under IFRS. Accounting for transaction costs and contingent consideration differs under IFRS.	2	Goodwill is not amortised under IFRS. Accounting for transaction costs and contingent consideration differs under IFRS.
Discontinued operations and assets held for sale	2	Different definitions for discontinued operations. No concept of assets held for sale in either GAAP.	3	FRS 3 differs from IFRS 5.	3	FRS 102 does not deal with assets held for sale.
Investments in associates	1		1		1	
Investments in joint ventures (IFRS 11)	1		1		1	
Related-party transactions	1	Similar definitions and disclosures.	1	Similar definitions and disclosures.	1	Similar definitions and disclosures.
Specialised activities (agriculture)	2	Cost or fair value policy choice under FRS 102. No specific guidance under old UK GAAP.	3	No fair value standard under old UK GAAP.	2	Cost or fair value policy choice under FRS 102. IFRS requires fair values.
Service concession arrangements	3	FRS 102 includes an intangible asset model for operators.	3	Old UK GAAP covers accounting by grantors. IFRS includes an intangible asset model for operators.	2	FRS 102 covers accounting by grantors.

Key:

1	Same or minor differences
2	Some differences
3	Significant differences

1. Accounting rules and principles

Accounting framework

	Old UK GAAP	New UK GAAP (FRS 102)	IFRS
Scope	Applies to all entities. Accounting standards are applicable to financial statements of a reporting entity that are intended to give a true and fair view of its state of affairs at the balance sheet date and of its profit or loss (or income and expenditure) for the financial period ending on that date. [Foreword to accounting standards, para 13].	Applies to financial statements that are intended to give a true and fair view of a reporting entity's financial position and profit or loss (or income and expenditure) for a period. It applies to public benefit entities and other entities, not just to companies. Consolidated financial statements of entities listed on a regulated market in the EU must apply EU-adopted IFRS and not FRS 102. A qualifying entity (subsidiaries and parents for their individual accounts) can choose to apply the reduced disclosures in FRS 101. [FRS 100 paras 2, 4].	Applies to all entities. IFRSs are developed and published to promote the use of IFRSs in general purpose financial statements and other financial reporting. IFRSs apply to all general purpose financial statements, which are directed towards the common information needs of a wide range of users. [Preface to IFRS, paras 7, 10].
Small entities	Accounting for small entities is covered by the small companies regime in company law and the FRSSE. Small entities are not covered in this publication.	Accounting for small entities is covered by the small companies regime in company law and by FRS 102, including Section 1A on presentation and disclosure requirements, or, for micro-entities, by FRS 105.	Accounting for small entities is covered by the IFRS for SMEs (but this does not apply for UK reporters).
Definitions			
Asset	Assets are rights or other access to future economic benefits controlled by an entity as a result of past transactions or events. Although assets commonly have other features that help identify them (for example, they may be acquired at a cost and they may be tangible, exchangeable or legally enforceable), those features are not essential characteristics of an asset; their absence is not sufficient in itself to preclude an item from qualifying as an asset. [Statement of principles for financial reporting (SoP), paras 4.6–4.7].	An asset is a resource controlled by an entity as a result of past events and from which future economic benefits are expected to flow to the entity. Future economic benefits can arise from continuing use of the asset or from its disposal. The following factors are not essential in assessing the existence of an asset: • Its physical substance. • The right of ownership. [FRS 102 paras 2.15(a), 2.17-2.19].	Same as new UK GAAP. [IFRS Framework paras 4.4(a), 4.8-4.14].

	Old UK GAAP	New UK GAAP (FRS 102)	IFRS
Liability	Liabilities are obligations of an entity to transfer economic benefits as a result of past transactions or events.	A liability is a present obligation of an entity arising from past events, the settlement of which is expected to result in an outflow from the entity of resources embodying economic benefits.	Same as new UK GAAP. [IFRS Framework paras 4.4(b), 4.15-4.19].
	Although many liabilities are based on legal obligations, a legal obligation is not a necessary condition: a liability can exist in the absence of legal obligations if commercial considerations create a constructive obligation. [SoP paras 4.23, 4.26].	The present obligation can be either a legal or constructive obligation (based on an established pattern of past practice or the creation of valid expectations). [FRS 102 paras 2.15(b), 2.20–2.21].	
Equity	Ownership interest or equity is defined as the residual amount found by deducting all of the entity's liabilities from all of its assets. [SoP para 4.37].	Similar to old UK GAAP. Equity is the residual interest in the entity's assets after deducting all of its liabilities. Equity includes: • investments by the owners of the entity; • plus additions to those investments earned through profitable operations and retained for use in the entity's operations; • less reductions to owner's investments as a result of unprofitable operations and distributions to owners. [FRS 102 paras 2.22, 22.3].	Similar to new UK GAAP. Equity is the residual interest in the assets of the entity after deducting all liabilities. [IFRS Glossary].
Income	Income and gains are increases in ownership interest not resulting from contributions from owners. [SoP para 4.39].	Similar to old UK GAAP. 'Income' is increases in economic benefits during the reporting period in the form of inflows or enhancements of assets; or decreases in liabilities that result in increases in equity, other than those relating to contributions from equity investors. [FRS 102 para 2.23(a)].	Same as new UK GAAP. [IFRS Framework para 4.25(a)].
Expenses	Expenses (losses) are decreases in ownership interest not resulting from distributions to owners. [SoP paras 4.39-4.40].	Similar to old UK GAAP. Expenses are decreases in economic benefits during the reporting period in the form of outflows or depletions of assets or incurrences of liabilities that result in decreases in equity, other than those relating to distributions to equity investors. [FRS 102 para 2.23(b)].	Same as new UK GAAP. [IFRS Framework para 4.25(b)].

	Old UK GAAP	New UK GAAP (FRS 102)	IFRS
Recognition of the elements of the financial statements	If a transaction or other event has created a new asset or liability (or added to an existing asset or liability), that effect is recognised if: • sufficient evidence exists that the new asset or liability has been created (or that there has been an addition to an existing asset or liability); and • the new asset or liability (or the addition to the existing asset or liability) can be measured at a monetary amount with sufficient reliability. In a transaction involving the provision of services or goods for a net gain, the recognition criteria described above will be met on the occurrence of the critical event in the operating cycle involved. Where a net loss is expected, this is recognised immediately. [SoP paras 5.14, 5.17, 5.26-5.27, 5.33-5.36].	Recognition is the process of incorporating, in the balance sheet or statement of comprehensive income, an item that meets the definition of an element and satisfies the following criteria: • it is probable that any future economic benefit associated with the items will flow to or from the entity; and • cost or value can be measured reliably. A failure to recognise an item that satisfies these criteria is not rectified by disclosure of accounting policies used or by notes or explanatory materials. An item that fails to meet the recognition criteria may qualify for recognition at a later date as a result of subsequent circumstances or events. [FRS 102 paras 2.27-2.32].	Same as new UK GAAP. [IFRS Framework paras 4.37-4.43].
Concepts and pervasive principles			
Measurement bases	The measurement bases include historical cost and current value. The basis selected is the one that best meets the objective of financial statements. The current value can be determined by reference to the entry price (replacement cost), exit value (net realisable value) or value in use (discounted cash flows). [SoP paras 6.1, 6.6].	Items are usually accounted for at their historical cost. However, certain items are carried at fair value – for example, categories of financial instruments, investment property, agricultural assets, property, plant and equipment (if the revaluation model is used) and investments in associates and joint ventures (if an entity measures these at fair value). All items other than those carried at fair value through profit or loss are subject to impairment tests and are presented net of any accumulated impairment losses. [FRS 102 paras 2.46-2.51]. In the absence of any specific guidance in the relevant section of FRS 102, the guidance in section 11 is used in determining fair value. [FRS 102 para 2.34].	The measurement bases include historical cost, current cost, realisable value and present value. The measurement basis most commonly adopted is historical cost. However, certain items are valued at fair value (for example, investment property, biological assets and certain categories of financial instrument). [IFRS Framework paras 4.55-4.56].
Underlying assumptions	*Accruals concept:* transactions or other events, as far as possible, should be reflected in the financial statements in the accounting period in which they occur.	Financial statements are prepared on an accrual basis and on the assumption that the entity is a going concern and will continue in operation in the foreseeable future (which is at least, but not limited to, 12 months from the date when the	Same as new UK GAAP, although the future period for going concern purposes is at least (but not limited to) 12 months from the end of the reporting period. [IAS 1 paras 25, 27].

	Old UK GAAP	New UK GAAP (FRS 102)	IFRS
	Going concern assumption: financial statements are prepared on the assumption that the entity is to continue in operational existence for the foreseeable future. [SoP paras 3.6, 5.6-5.7; FRS 18 paras 21, 26].	financial statements are authorised for issue). [FRS 102 paras 2.36, 3.8].	
Qualitative characteristics	The qualitative characteristics are relevance, reliability, comparability and understandability.	The principal qualitative characteristics (that make the information provided in financial statements useful to users) are understandability, relevance, materiality, reliability, substance over form, prudence, completeness, comparability, timeliness and achieving a balance between benefit and cost.	There are two fundamental qualitative characteristics of financial statements that are needed if the financial information is to be useful: relevance, and faithful representation.
	In addition, materiality is considered a threshold quality to determine if information is of such significance as to require its inclusion in the financial statements.	Information is material if its omission or misstatement, individually or collectively, could influence the economic decisions of users taken on the basis of the financial statements. Materiality depends on the size and nature of the omission or misstatement judged in the surrounding circumstances. The size or nature of the item, or a combination of both, could be the determining factor. [FRS 102 paras 2.4-2.14].	Materiality is a sub-principle of relevance.
	Faithful representation, neutrality, being complete and free from material error and prudence are sub-characteristics of reliability. Consistency and disclosure of accounting policies are sub-characteristics of comparability. Information is material if its misstatement or omission might reasonably be expected to influence the economic decisions of the users of the financial statements. [SoP paras 3.1-3.7].		Characteristics of faithful representation are for information to be complete, neutral and free from error. Furthermore the usefulness of financial information is enhanced if it is comparable, verifiable, timely and understandable. [Framework paras QC4– QC32].
True and fair view/Fair presentation	Financial statements are required to give a true and fair view of the financial performance and financial position of the entity.	Financial statements should give a true and fair view of the assets, liabilities, financial position, financial performance and, when required to be presented, cash flows of an entity. This is achieved by applying the appropriate section of FRS 102 and the principal qualitative characteristics outlined above. [FRS 102 para 3.2].	Fair presentation requires the faithful representation of the effects of transactions, other events and conditions in accordance with the definitions and recognition criteria for assets, liabilities, income and expenses set out in the Framework. [IAS 1 paras15-16].

	Old UK GAAP	New UK GAAP (FRS 102)	IFRS
	In exceptional circumstances, entities are permitted to depart from the standards in order to give a true and fair view. In such circumstances, additional explanations and disclosures should be provided. In practice, most true and fair overrides relate to Companies Act legislation rather than accounting standards. [SoP, introduction para 7; FRS 18 para 15].	In special circumstances, entities are permitted to depart from FRS 102 (or from applicable legislation if it allows for a true and fair override) only if management concludes that compliance with a requirement is inconsistent with the requirement to give a true and fair view. The nature and effect of the departure, and the reason for it, are explained in the financial statements. [FRS 102 paras 3.4-3.5].	Entities are permitted to depart from IFRS, but this is rare in practice. [IAS 1 paras 19-20].
Offsetting	Assets and liabilities can only be offset if the company has the ability to insist on the net settlement of the balances. [SoP para 4.34].	Assets and liabilities or income and expenses cannot be offset, except where specifically required or permitted by the standard. [FRS 102 para 2.52].	Same as new UK GAAP. [IAS para 1 para 32].

First-time adoption

	Old UK GAAP	New UK GAAP (FRS 102)	IFRS
Transition to new UK GAAP/ IFRS	Not applicable.	A first-time adopter is an entity that presents its first annual financial statements under FRS 102, regardless of whether its previous accounting framework was IFRS or another set of generally accepted accounting principles.	A first-time adopter of IFRS is an entity that presents its first annual financial statements that conform to IFRS.
		First-time adoption requires full retrospective application of FRS 102 effective at the reporting date for an entity's first new UK GAAP financial statements. There are a number of mandatory exceptions and optional exemptions in section 35 of FRS 102, and a general exemption on the grounds of impracticability regarding retrospective application. [FRS 102 paras 35.1, 35.9–35.11].	Similar exceptions and exemptions to those in new UK GAAP. The differences are explained below. [IFRS 1 paras 2, 4, 7, 10, Appendices B, C, D].
		Section 35 permits repeated application. An entity that has previously applied FRS 102, but whose most recent annual financial statements did not contain a statement of compliance with the FRS, has a choice of applying (i) section 35, or (ii) FRS 102 retrospectively in accordance with section 10 as if the entity had never stopped applying the FRS. [FRS 102 para 35.2].	IFRS 1 permits repeated application. An entity that has applied IFRSs in the past, but whose most recent financial statements did not contain a statement of compliance with IFRSs, must either apply IFRS 1 or else apply IFRSs retrospectively under IAS 8. [IFRS 1 para 4A].

	Old UK GAAP	New UK GAAP (FRS 102)	IFRS
Date of transition	Not applicable.	This is the beginning of the earliest period for which full comparative information is presented in accordance with new UK GAAP in an entity's first new UK GAAP financial statements. [FRS 102 para 35.6].	Same as new UK GAAP. [IFRS 1 App A].
Reconciliation	Not applicable.	A first-time adopter's first financial statements include the following: • reconciliations of its equity reported under its previous financial reporting framework to its equity under new UK GAAP for both the transition date and the end of the latest period presented in the entity's most recent annual financial statements under its previous financial reporting framework; • a reconciliation of the profit or loss reported under its previous financial reporting framework for the latest period in its most recent annual financial statements to its profit or loss under new UK GAAP for the same period; and • correction of errors made under previous GAAP, separately disclosed. [FRS 102 paras 35.13-35.14].	Similar to new UK GAAP, additional information regarding impairment losses on transition is required. [IFRS 1 paras 23-28].
Opening balance sheet for prior period	Not applicable.	A first-time adopter has to prepare an opening balance sheet at the date of transition to FRS 102, but there is no requirement to present it. [FRS 102 para 35.7].	A first-time adopter has to prepare and present an opening balance sheet (and related notes) at the date of transition to IFRS. [IFRS 1 paras 6, 21]. *FRS 101 RDF (IFRS): A first-time adopter is not required to present an opening balance sheet at the date of transition. [FRS 100 para 11(b); FRS 101 para 7A].*
Mandatory exceptions	Not applicable.	A first-time adopter does not change the accounting that it followed previously for any of the following transactions: • derecognition of financial assets and liabilities; • accounting estimates; • discontinued operations; and • measuring non-controlling interests. [FRS 102 para 35.9].	Similar to new UK GAAP, although there are further exceptions for government loans; classification and measurement of financial assets; hedge accounting and embedded derivatives. Also, there is no exception for discontinued operations. [IFRS 1 App B].

	Old UK GAAP	New UK GAAP (FRS 102)	IFRS
Optional exemptions	Not applicable.	The following optional exemptions from the requirement for retrospective application are available for use if they are relevant to the entity: • business combinations (FRS 102 specifies that this includes group reconstructions); • share-based payment transactions (but a first-time adopter previously applying FRS 20 or IFRS 2 can apply either of those standards (as applicable) or Section 26 of FRS 102 for equity share-based payment transactions at the date of transition); • fair value as deemed cost for PPE, investment property or intangible asset; • revaluation as deemed cost for PPE, investment property or intangible asset; • investments in subsidiaries, associates and jointly controlled entities (in separate financial statements); • compound financial instruments; • service concession arrangements; • extractive activities; • arrangements containing a lease; • decommissioning liabilities included in the cost of PPE; • dormant companies – allowing these to retain accounting policies until there is a change to relevant balances, or new transactions are entered into; • deferred development costs as a deemed cost; • capitalisation of borrowing costs; • lease incentives; • public benefit entity combinations; • transition date for assets and liabilities of subsidiaries, associates and joint ventures; • designation of previously recognised debt instruments; and	Most of the exemptions available in new UK GAAP are also available on transitioning to IFRS, except for the exemptions related to: • extractive activities; • dormant companies; • deferred development costs as a deemed cost; • lease incentives; • public benefit entity combinations; • hedge accounting (there is an exception under IFRS 1); and • small entities. IFRS also includes exemptions for: • insurance contracts; • employee benefits; • cumulative translation differences; • fair value measurement of financial assets and liabilities at initial recognition; • transfers of assets from customers; • extinguishing financial liabilities with equity instruments; • severe hyperinflation; • joint arrangements; • stripping costs in the production phase of a surface mine; and • regulatory deferral accounts (IFRS 14). [IFRS 1 Appendices C, D, IFRS 14]. *FRS 101 RDF (IFRS): The first-time adoption exemption (in paras D16 and D17 of IFRS 1) for parents, subsidiaries, joint ventures and associates' individual financial statements is restricted to situations where measuring assets and liabilities in the individual financial statements based on figures in the consolidated financial statements would*

	Old UK GAAP	New UK GAAP (FRS 102)	IFRS
		• hedge accounting. Also, additional transitional exemptions for small entities have been added to FRS 102 in the July 2015 amendments, covering: • share-based payment; • fair value measurement of financial instruments; • financing transactions involving related parties. [FRS 102 para 35.10].	*comply with FRS 101 (including company law). [FRS 101 para AG1(a),(b)].*
Subsequent application of exemptions	Not applicable.	FRS 102 makes it clear that, where the above exemptions have been applied at the date of transition, they can continue to be used in subsequent financial statements until the related assets and liabilities are derecognised. But, if there is a significant change in circumstances, an entity should reassess the appropriateness of applying an exemption in order to give a true and fair view in accordance with section 3 of FRS 102. [FRS 102 paras 35.11A, 35.11B].	Not referred to in IFRS.
General exemption	Not applicable.	If it is impracticable for a first-time adopter to restate the opening balance sheet at the date of transition for one or more of the adjustments required by new UK GAAP, the adjustments are applied in the earliest period for which it is practicable to do so. If it is impracticable for a first-time adopter to provide disclosures required by FRS 102 for any comparative period, the omission is disclosed. [FRS 102 para 35.11].	Not applicable.
Transition adjustments	Not applicable.	Adjustments arising on transition to new UK GAAP relating to transactions, other events or conditions before the date of transition are recognised directly in retained earnings (or, if appropriate, another category of equity) at the date of transition. [FRS 102 para 35.8].	Same as new UK GAAP. [IFRS 1 para 11].

Financial statements

Sections 3 to 8 of FRS 102 set the requirements for the presentation of financial statements for entities not using section 1A for small entities, including guidelines for their structure, and minimum requirements for their content. These are based on company law, which sets the main requirements for presentation of financial statements under UK GAAP, including the formats for the primary statements. Where permitted by the law, entities have a choice of using detailed company law formats or adapting the formats as set out in FRS 102 (under the July 2015 amendments).

	Old UK GAAP	New UK GAAP (FRS 102)	IFRS
General requirements			
Compliance	Financial statements disclose whether they have been prepared in accordance with applicable accounting standards. Any material departure is disclosed and explained. [SI 2008/410 1 Sch 45; FRS 18 para 62].	Management explicitly states that financial statements comply with FRS 102. Compliance cannot be claimed unless the financial statements comply with all the requirements of the standard. [FRS 102 para 3.3].	Similar to new UK GAAP, as all requirements of IFRS must be complied with. [IAS 1 para 16].
Going concern	Financial statements are prepared on the assumption that the entity is a going concern and will continue in operation for the foreseeable future. An entity is a going concern unless management either intends to liquidate the entity or to cease operations, or has no realistic alternative but to do so. [FRS 18 paras 21, 61].	Similar to old UK GAAP, except that the foreseeable future is at least 12 months from the date when the financial statements are approved for issue. [FRS 102 paras 3.8-3.9].	Same as new UK GAAP, except that the foreseeable future is at least 12 months from the reporting date. [IAS 1 paras 25-26].
Departure from the standard	Management departs from the standard if it concludes that compliance with the requirement would be inconsistent with the requirement to give a true and fair view. In such circumstances, additional disclosures are provided. Departures from standards are rare in practice.	In special circumstances, management departs from the standard if it concludes that compliance with the requirement is inconsistent with the requirement to give a true and fair view. Where management departs from a requirement of FRS 102 or from a requirement of applicable legislation (where permitted), specific disclosure requirements apply. [FRS 102 paras 3.4-3.5].	Similar to new UK GAAP. Management may not depart from the standard if the relevant regulatory framework prohibits the departure. [IAS 1 paras 19, 20]. Departures from standards are rare in practice.
Comparative information	Management discloses comparative information in respect of the previous comparable period for all amounts reported in the primary financial statements and notes, except where an FRS permits or requires otherwise. [FRS 28 paras 6, 10, 11].	Same as old UK GAAP. Comparatives are disclosed except where FRS 102 permits or requires otherwise. [FRS 102 para 3.14]. For example FRS 102 para 17.31 does not require a prior period reconciliation of the movements in property, plant and equipment.	Same as new UK GAAP. Comparatives are disclosed except where IFRS permits or requires otherwise. [IAS 1 para 38]. *FRS 101 RDF (IFRS): FRS 101 has an exemption from the requirement to present comparatives in various roll-forward reconciliations, including movements in share capital (IAS 1), property, plant and equipment (IAS 16), intangible assets (IAS 38), investment property (IAS 40) and biological assets (IAS 41). [FRS 101 para 8(f)].*

	Old UK GAAP	New UK GAAP (FRS 102)	IFRS
Opening balance sheet for prior period	Not applicable.	Not applicable.	See next section on components of financial statements.
Components of financial statements	A set of financial statements comprises: • a balance sheet [Company law]; • a profit and loss account [Company law]; • a statement of total recognised gain and losses [FRS 3 para 27]; • a cash flow statement (although certain entities are exempt) [FRS 1 para 5]; and • notes, including a summary of the significant accounting policies and estimations. [FRS 18 para 55].	A complete set of financial statements comprises: • a statement of financial position (also referred to as a balance sheet); • a single statement of comprehensive income (including items of other comprehensive income), or a separate income statement and a separate statement of comprehensive income; • a statement of changes in equity; • a statement of cash flows (when required to be presented); and • notes, comprising a summary of significant accounting policies and other explanatory information. Under certain circumstances, the statements under the second and third bullets may be combined into one statement of income and retained earnings. An entity may use other titles for these statements, provided they are not misleading. [FRS 102 paras 3.17-3.22]. The July 2015 amendments to FRS 102 introduce Section 1A setting out the information to be presented in the financial statements of a small entity that chooses to apply the small entities regime, and also withdraw the FRSSE.	Similar to new UK GAAP, although IFRS does not permit a single statement of 'income and retained earnings'. The entity may use titles for the statements other than those used in IAS 1, 'Presentation of financial statements'. In addition, a statement of financial position as at the beginning of the earliest comparative period is included where an entity applies an accounting policy retrospectively or makes a retrospective restatement, or where it reclassifies items in its financial statements. [IAS 1 para 10]. *FRS 101 RDF (IFRS): FRS 101 has an exemption from the requirement to present a balance sheet as at the beginning of the preceding period if there is a prior year adjustment. [FRS 101 para 8(g)].*
Statement of financial position (balance sheet)			
General	There is no UK accounting standard dealing with presentation. However, the required format of separate company and consolidated group financial statements is laid down in regulations. [Companies Act 2006; SI 2008/409; SI 2008/410; UITF 4].	An entity presents a balance sheet in line with the formats for separate company or group financial statements set out in regulations. This applies to all entities, whether or not they report under the Companies Act, unless the requirements are not permitted by any statutory framework under which such entities report. [FRS 102 paras 4.1-4.2].	IAS 1 specifies the minimum line items that should be included on the face of the balance sheet. [IAS 1 para 54]. *FRS 101 RDF (IFRS): Where the detailed company law formats apply, the primary statement formats in IAS 1 cannot be used unless they comply with the formats in the regulations. If there are differences, the company law formats have to be used. However, the July 2015 amendments to*

	Old UK GAAP	New UK GAAP (FRS 102)	IFRS
		The July 2015 amendments to FRS 102 allow a company to adapt the company law formats and specify minimum disclosures. [FRS 102 para 4.2A].	*FRS 101 reflect changes in company law allowing the use of IFRS-based presentation standards for the balance sheet where entities choose (and are permitted) to adapt company law formats. [FRS 101 para AG1(h)].*
Current/non-current distinction	Company law mandates the format and presentation of the financial statements. Fixed assets, current assets, creditors due within one year, creditors due after more than one year, and provisions are all separately disclosed. Non-current debtors are included within current assets, but they are separately disclosed in the balance sheet or in the notes. [Companies Act 2006; SI 2008/409; SI 2008/410; UITF 4].	*Detailed company law formats* Same as old UK GAAP where the detailed company law formats are used. Also, in that case, FRS 102 specifies that an entity classifies a liability as due within one year where the entity does not have an unconditional right to defer settlement of the liability for at least 12 months after the reporting date. [FRS 102 para 4.7]. *Adapted formats* There are separate definitions (based on IFRS) for entities that are adapting the formats under the July 2015 amendments to FRS 102, such that the requirements are the same as IFRS. [FRS 102 App 1 Glossary].	A current/non-current distinction is required, except where a liquidity presentation is more relevant. An asset is classified as current if it is: • expected to be realised, sold or consumed in the entity's normal operating cycle; • primarily held for the purpose of trading; • expected to be realised within 12 months after the balance sheet date; or • cash or a cash equivalent (that is not restricted in use for at least 12 months after the balance sheet date). An entity classifies all other assets as non-current. A liability is classified as current if: • it is expected to be settled in the entity's normal operating cycle; • it is primarily held for the purpose of trading; • it is expected to be settled within 12 months after the balance sheet date; or • the entity does not have an unconditional right to defer settlement of the liability until 12 months after the balance sheet date. An entity classifies all other liabilities as non-current. [IAS 1 paras 60, 66, 69]. *FRS 101 RDF (IFRS): Where the detailed company law formats are used, this means showing fixed assets rather than non-current assets (that is, different definitions). Also, the liquidity presentation cannot be used, as it does not comply*

	Old UK GAAP	New UK GAAP (FRS 102)	IFRS
			with company law. However, as noted above, the July 2015 amendments to FRS 101 reflect changes in company law and permit the use of IFRS-based presentation standards.
Profit and loss account, statement of total recognised gains and losses (income statement and statement of comprehensive income)			
General	There is no UK accounting standard dealing with the layout of the primary financial statements; however, FRS 3 requires the presentation of a 'statement of total recognised gains and losses'. In addition, the required format of separate company and consolidated group financial statements is laid down in statutory instruments supporting company law. Company law allows the use of two formats for the profit and loss account presentation: format 1 is similar to the 'function' method under IFRS; and format 2 is similar to the 'nature' method. [Companies Act 2006; SI 2008/409; SI 2008/410; UITF 4].	An entity is required to present a statement of comprehensive income, either in a single statement or in two statements comprising a separate income statement and a statement of comprehensive income. Entities that meet specified conditions can elect to present a combined statement of income and retained earnings. [FRS 102 paras 5.1, 5.2]. The income statement (or the similar section of a single statement of comprehensive income) is presented in line with the profit and loss accounts formats for separate company or group financial statements set out in statutory instruments. This applies to all entities, whether or not they report under the Companies Act, unless the requirements are not permitted by any statutory framework under which such entities report. [FRS 102 paras 5.1, 5.5, 5.7]. The July 2015 amendments to FRS 102 allow a company to adapt the company law formats and specify minimum disclosures. [FRS 102 para 5.5B]. Management selects a method of presenting its expenses by either function or nature. Additional disclosure of expenses by nature is required if presentation by function is chosen. [FRS 102 para 5.11].	Same as new UK GAAP. [IAS 1 paras 81-83]. *FRS 101 RDF (IFRS): Where the detailed company law formats apply, the primary statement formats in IAS 1 cannot be used unless they comply with the formats in the regulations. If there are differences, the company law formats have to be used. However, the July 2015 amendments to FRS 101 reflect changes in company law allowing the use of IFRS-based presentation standards for the income statement where entities choose (and are permitted) to adapt company law formats. In addition, 'profit or loss before tax' has to be disclosed. [FRS 101 para AG1(i)].* *Also, IAS 1 is amended by FRS 101 to comply with the requirement in company law that generally only realised profits are included in profit or loss (subject to the exceptions under the Act's fair value accounting rules). Items of income and expense arising in a period are recognised in profit or loss, unless an IFRS requires or permits otherwise, or unless prohibited by the Act. [FRS 101 para AG1(k)].*
Line items	Company law prescribes the line items to be presented in the profit and loss account. FRS 3 requires additional line items (such as operating profit) to be disclosed. [Companies Act 2006; SI 2008/409; SI 2008/410; UITF 4].	The income statement (or the similar section of a single statement of comprehensive income) follows the company law formats, or under the July 2015 amendments to FRS 102, the adapted formats set out in FRS 102.	The following items are required to be presented in the income statement (or the similar section of a single statement of comprehensive income) as a minimum: • revenue; • finance costs;

	Old UK GAAP	New UK GAAP (FRS 102)	IFRS

	A primary statement is presented with the same prominence as the other primary statements, showing the total of recognised gains and losses and its components. The components are the gains and losses that are recognised in the period, insofar as they are attributable to shareholders. [FRS 3 para 27].	Disclosure of 'operating profit' is not required. However, if an entity elects to disclose this, it should ensure that the amount disclosed is representative of activities that would normally be regarded as 'operating'.
		
		In addition, an entity includes the following line items in the statement of comprehensive income (under both the single and two-statement approaches):
		• each item of other comprehensive income classified by nature;
		• share of the other comprehensive income of associates and jointly controlled entities accounted for by the equity method; and
		• total comprehensive income.
		
		Profit or loss for the period and total comprehensive income for the period are allocated in the statement of comprehensive income to the amounts attributable to non-controlling interests and owners of the parent. [FRS 102 paras 5.5-5.7A, 5.9B].
			• share of profit or loss of associates and joint ventures accounted for using the equity method;
			• tax expense;
			• a single item comprising the total of:
			  • the post-tax gain or loss of discontinued operations; and
			  • the post-tax gain or loss recognised on the measurement to fair value less costs to sell, or on the disposal of the assets or disposal group(s) constituting the discontinued operation; and
			• profit or loss for the period.
			
			The presentation of items of other comprehensive income in the statement of comprehensive income (under both the single and two-statement approaches) is the same as under new UK GAAP, except in one respect: IFRS also requires that those items are analysed between those that will be reclassified subsequently to profit or loss, and those that will not. [IAS 1 para 82A].
			
			As under new UK GAAP, profit or loss for the period, and total comprehensive income for the period, are allocated in the statement of comprehensive income to the amounts attributable to non-controlling interests and to the owners of the parent. [IAS 1 paras 82-83].

Exceptional items	FRS 3 defines exceptional items as material items arising from ordinary activity that need to be disclosed separately (by virtue of size or incidence) if the financial statements are to give a true and fair view. It identifies three categories of exceptional item that are required to be shown after operating profit. Other exceptional items are disclosed in arriving at operating profit. [FRS 3 paras 18-19].	Exceptional items are not defined. However, each material class of items is presented separately, and additional line items are presented where they are relevant to an understanding of financial performance. [FRS 102 paras 3.15, 5.9, 5.9A].	Same as new UK GAAP. [IAS 1 para 97].

	Old UK GAAP	New UK GAAP (FRS 102)	IFRS
Extraordinary items	Any extraordinary item is shown separately in the profit and loss account. Extraordinary items are extremely rare in practice. [FRS 3 paras 22, 48].	Extraordinary items do not occur in practice. In any case, under the July 2015 amendments to FRS 102, extraordinary items are removed from the formats for companies reporting under Schedule 1 to SI 2008/410.	Extraordinary items are not presented. [IAS 1 para 87].
Statement of changes in equity			

General	FRS 3 requires a reconciliation of movements in shareholders' funds, disclosing movements in share capital and reserves, either in a note or on the face of the financial statements. [FRS 3 para 28].	The statement of changes in equity presents a reconciliation of equity items between the beginning and end of the period.
		
		The following items are presented on the face of the statement of changes in equity:
		• total comprehensive income for the period;
		• for each component of equity, the effects of changes in accounting policies and corrections of material prior-period errors; and
		• for each component of equity, reconciliation between the carrying amount at the beginning and the end of the period, separately disclosing changes resulting from:
		  • profit or loss;
		  • other comprehensive income; and
		  • the amount of investments by, and dividends and other distributions to, owners.
		
		For each component of equity, an entity should present, either in the statement of changes in equity or in the notes, an analysis of other comprehensive income by item. [FRS 102 paras 6.3-6.3A].
			Same as new UK GAAP. [IAS 1 para 106].
			
			The amounts of dividends recognised as distributions to owners during the period, and the related amount per share, are presented either in the statement of changes in equity or in the notes. [IAS 1 para 107].

Combined statement of income and retained earnings	Not applicable.	A combined statement of income and retained earnings can be presented, instead of a statement of comprehensive income and a statement of changes in equity, if the only changes to an entity's equity during the period are a result of profit or loss, payment of dividends, correction of material prior-period errors, or changes in accounting policy.	Not permitted.

	Old UK GAAP	New UK GAAP (FRS 102)	IFRS
		In addition to the line items required in the statement of comprehensive income, the following items are presented in the combined statement of income and retained earnings: • retained earnings at the start of the period; • dividends declared and paid or payable during the period; • restatement of retained earnings for correction of material prior-period errors; • restatement of retained earnings for changes in accounting policy; and • retained earnings at the end of the period. [FRS 102 paras 6.4-6.5].	
Cash flow statement (Statement of cash flows)			
Scope	Some entities are exempt from presenting a cash flow statement, including small entities and subsidiary undertakings where 90% or more of the voting rights are controlled within the group, provided that the subsidiary is included in publicly available consolidated financial statements. [FRS 1 para 5].	A qualifying entity (that is, an entity included in publicly available consolidated financial statements that give a true and fair view) is exempt from presenting a cash flow statement. [FRS 102 para 1.12(a)]. An exemption also applies for: a. Mutual life assurance companies. b. Retirement benefit plans. c. Open-ended investment funds that meet specified criteria. [FRS 102 para 7.1A]. A further exemption for small entities was added in the July 2015 amendments to FRS 102. [FRS 102 para 7.1B]. This exemption applies even if the entity chooses not to apply the small entities regime in section 1A of FRS 102.	No exemptions are available under IFRS from the requirement to present the statement of cash flows. [IAS 7 para 1]. *FRS 101 RDF (IFRS): Qualifying entities are not required to present a cash flow statement. [FRS 101 para 8(h)].*
Content	The cash flow statement includes all of the reporting entity's inflows and outflows of 'cash' for the period. [FRS 1 para 6]. 'Cash' comprises cash on hand and demand deposits.	The cash flow statement includes all of the reporting entity's inflows and outflows of cash and 'cash equivalents' for the period. [FRS 102 para 7.1].	Same as new UK GAAP. [IAS 7 para 6].

	Old UK GAAP	New UK GAAP (FRS 102)	IFRS
		'Cash equivalents' are short-term, highly liquid investments that are readily convertible to known amounts of cash and that are subject to insignificant risk of changes in value. [FRS 102 para 7.2, Glossary].	
Format	Cash flows are classified under the following headings: • operating activities; • dividends from joint ventures and associates; • returns on investment and servicing of finance; • taxation; • capital expenditure and financial investments; • acquisitions and disposals; • equity dividends paid; • management of liquid resources; and • financing. [FRS 1 para 7].	Cash flows are classified under the following standard headings: • operating activities; • investing activities; and • financing activities. [FRS 102 paras 7.3-7.6].	Same as new UK GAAP. [IAS 7 paras 10-17].
	A note reconciling the movement of cash in the period with the movement in net debt is provided, either adjoining the cash flow statement or in a note. [FRS 1 para 33].	A reconciliation of net debt is not required. [FRS 102 para 7.20].	Same as new UK GAAP. [IAS 7 para 45].
Reporting cash flow from operating activities	Operating cash flows are presented by either the direct method (showing the relevant constituent cash flows) or the indirect method (calculating operating cash flows by adjustment to the operating profit reported in the profit and loss account). [FRS 1 para 7].	Operating cash flows are presented by using either the direct method (gross cash receipts and payments) or the indirect method (adjusting 'profit or loss' for non-operating and non-cash transactions, and for changes in working capital). [FRS 102 para 7.7].	Same as new UK GAAP. The direct method is encouraged. [IAS 7 paras 18-20, 22].
Reporting cash flow from investing and financing activities	Cash flows are presented gross, except in some limited instances. Cash inflows and outflows within the management of liquid resources or financing may also be netted against each other if they either (a) relate in substance to a single financing transaction, or (b) are due to short maturities and high turnover occurring from rollover or reissue. [FRS 1 para 8].	Similar to old UK GAAP. Cash flows from major classes of investing and financing activities are reported separately and gross. Cash flows from investing and financing activities may be reported on a net basis if they relate to items in which the turnover is quick, the amounts are large and the maturities are short. [FRS 102 paras 7.10, 7.10A, 7.10C].	Same as new UK GAAP. [IAS 7 paras 21-24].

	Old UK GAAP	New UK GAAP (FRS 102)	IFRS
		Financial institutions may report cash flows on a net basis [FRS 102 paras 7.10D, 7.10E].	
Non-cash transactions	Disclosure of significant non-cash transactions is required. [FRS 1 para 46].	Same as old UK GAAP. [FRS 102 paras 7.18-7.19].	Same as new UK GAAP. [IAS 7 paras 43-44].
Foreign currency cash flows	The cash flow of a foreign subsidiary is translated on the basis used for translating the results in the consolidated profit and loss account (that is, using either the temporal or the closing rate method discussed in the foreign currencies section). [FRS 1 para 41].	Cash flows arising from transactions in foreign currencies are translated to the functional currency, using the exchange rate at the date of the cash flows or an average rate that approximates to the actual rate. Cash flows of a foreign subsidiary are translated using the exchange rate at the date of the cash flows or an average rate that approximates to the actual rate. Unrealised gains and losses arising from changes in foreign currency exchange rates are not cash flows. These gains and losses are presented separately from cash flows arising from operating, investing and financing activities. [FRS 102 paras 7.11 – 7.13].	Same as new UK GAAP. [IAS 7 paras 25-28].
Acquisitions and disposals of subsidiary undertakings	Material effects on the amounts reported under each of the standard headings, reflecting the cash flows of the subsidiary undertaking acquired or disposed of should be disclosed, as far as is practicable. [FRS 1 para 45].	No specific disclosure requirements.	Same as new UK GAAP.
Accounting policies, estimates and errors			
Selection of accounting policies and hierarchy of other guidance	An entity adopts accounting policies that enable its financial statements to give a true and fair view. The appropriateness of accounting policies is judged in terms of relevance, reliability, comparability and understandability. Old UK GAAP does not specify a hierarchy of guidance. [FRS 18 paras 14, 30-31].	Where an FRS or FRC Abstract does not address a transaction, other event or condition, management uses its judgement in developing and applying an accounting policy that results in information that is relevant and reliable. If there is no relevant guidance, management considers the following sources, in descending order: • the requirements and guidance in an FRS or FRC Abstract on similar and related issues;	Similar to new UK GAAP; however, management considers IFRS requirements on similar and related issues as a source of guidance. In addition, management may consider the most recent pronouncements of other standard-setting bodies, other accounting literature and accepted industry practices, to the extent that these do not conflict with the concepts in IFRS. With regard to the definitions, recognition criteria and measurement concepts for assets, liabilities, income and expenses, reference is made to the Framework. [IAS 8 paras 10-12].

	Old UK GAAP	**New UK GAAP (FRS 102)**	**IFRS**
		• where an entity is within a SORP's scope, the requirements and guidance in that SORP on similar and related issues; and • the definitions, recognition criteria and measurement concepts for assets, liabilities and income and expenses set out in section 2 of FRS 102. Management may also, but is not required to, consider EU-adopted IFRS. [FRS 102 paras 10.4-10.6].	
Consistency of accounting policies	Accounting policies are applied consistently to similar transactions. [FRS 18 para 39].	Similar to old UK GAAP. Accounting policies should be applied consistently for similar transactions, other events and conditions [FRS 102 para 10.7].	Same as new UK GAAP. [IAS 8 para 13].
Changes in accounting policies	Unless required otherwise by accounting standards or legislation, changes in accounting policies are applied retrospectively. [FRS 18 para 48].	Changes in accounting policies as a result of an amendment to an FRS or FRC Abstract are accounted for in accordance with the transitional provisions of that amendment. If specific transitional provisions do not exist, the changes are applied retrospectively. [FRS 102 para 10.11, 10.12].	Same as new UK GAAP. [IAS 8 para 19-27].
Changes in accounting estimates	Changes in accounting estimates are not treated as prior-period adjustments. [FRS 18 para 54].	Similar to old UK GAAP. Changes in accounting estimates are recognised prospectively by including the effects in profit or loss in the period that is affected (that is, the period of change and future periods), unless the change in estimates gives rise to changes in assets, liabilities or equity. In this case, it is recognised by adjusting the carrying amount of the related asset, liability or equity in the period of change. [FRS 102 paras 10.15-10.17].	Same as new UK GAAP. [IAS 8 paras 36-37].
Correction of prior-period errors	In exceptional circumstances, it may be found that financial statements of prior periods have been issued with errors that are of such significance as to destroy the 'true and fair view' and hence the validity of those financial statements. Such errors are considered 'fundamental'.	Errors may arise from mistakes and oversights or misinterpretation of available information. All 'material' prior-period errors are adjusted retrospectively (that is, by adjusting opening retained earnings and the related comparatives), unless it is impracticable to determine the effects of the error. (There is no concept of fundamental errors.) [FRS 102 paras 10.19-10.22].	Same as new UK GAAP. [IAS 8 paras 41-47].

	Old UK GAAP	New UK GAAP (FRS 102)	IFRS
	Prior-period errors that are 'fundamental' errors are accounted for retrospectively. All other prior-period errors are corrected prospectively. [FRS 18 para 34]. There are no exceptions from retrospective application where this is impracticable. [FRS 3 paras 7, 29, 60, 63].		
Notes to the financial statements			
General	The notes are an integral part of the financial statements. Notes provide additional information to the amounts disclosed in the primary statements. [Company law; FRS 18 para 55].	Same as old UK GAAP. [FRS 102 paras 8.1-8.2].	Same as new UK GAAP. [IAS 1 para 112].
Structure	The following disclosures are included, as a minimum, within the notes to the financial statements: • whether the financial statements have been prepared in accordance with applicable accounting standards; • a description of each material accounting policy; • a description of each material accounting estimate, including the estimation techniques; and • additional information that is necessary for financial statements to give a true and fair view. [Company law; FRS 18 paras 55, 57, 61, 62].	The following disclosures are included, as a minimum, within the notes to the financial statements: • a statement of compliance with FRS 102 [FRS 102 para 3.3]; • significant accounting policies; • information about judgements; • key sources of estimation uncertainty; • explanatory notes for items presented in the financial statements; and • information not presented in the primary statements. [FRS 102 paras 8.2-8.7]. Where applicable, the notes include disclosures of changes in accounting policies and of accounting estimates and of the correction of prior period errors. [FRS 102 paras 10.13, 10.14, 10.18, 10.23]. Consistent with the change in company law, the July 2015 amendments to FRS 102 require that the notes are presented in the order, where relevant, of the items in the statement of financial position and income statement to which they relate. [FRS 102 para 8.4 footnote].	Similar to new UK GAAP; however, IFRS generally has more extensive disclosure requirements, as well as a sensitivity analysis. Sensitivity analysis refers to disclosure of the impact or the sensitivity of the carrying amounts to the methods, assumptions and estimates underlying their calculation, including the reasons for the sensitivity. [IAS 1 paras 122, 125, 129].

	Old UK GAAP	New UK GAAP (FRS 102)	IFRS
Information about judgements	There is no explicit requirement to disclose information about judgements made in applying the accounting policies.	The judgements that management has made in applying the accounting policies, and that have the most significant effect on the amounts recognised in the financial statements, are disclosed in the notes. [FRS 102 para 8.6].	Same as new UK GAAP. [IAS 1 para 122].
Information about key sources of estimation uncertainty	A description is required of any significant estimation techniques. [FRS 18 paras 55, 57].	The nature and carrying amounts of assets and liabilities – for which estimates and assumptions have a significant risk of causing a material adjustment to their carrying amount within the next financial period – are disclosed in the notes. [FRS 102 para 8.7].	Similar to new UK GAAP. In addition, sensitivity analysis is given as an example of the type of disclosure that an entity makes. [IAS 1 para 125, 129].
Information about future standards	There is no requirement to give disclosure in respect of new standards and abstracts that have been issued but which are not yet effective.	Same as old UK GAAP.	IFRS requires disclosure in respect of new standards and interpretations that have been issued but which are not yet effective. [IAS 8 paras 30, 31]. *FRS 101 RDF (IFRS): Qualifying entities are exempt from this IAS 8 disclosure. [FRS 101 para 8(i)].*

Financial instruments

Under old UK GAAP, all entities apply FRS 25, which is based on the text of IAS 32 as at 31 March 2004, incorporating the revised version of IAS 32 issued by the IASB in December 2003; it also includes amendments made by IFRS 4, 'Insurance contracts'.

As explained below, not all old UK GAAP entities are required to apply FRS 26, which is based on the text of IAS 39 as at 31 March 2004, incorporating the revised version of IAS 39 issued by the IASB in December 2003, together with the amendments to IAS 39 on 'Fair value hedge accounting for a portfolio hedge of interest rate risk' and those made by IFRS 4, 'Insurance contracts', both issued in March 2004.

FRS 102 contains three sections addressing financial instruments: section 22 deals with the distinction between liabilities and equity; section 11 addresses the classification and measurement of simple payables and receivables and other basic financial instruments, and is relevant to all entities following FRS 102; and section 12 applies to other, more complex financial instruments and transactions, and contains provisions for hedge accounting. Section 12 is not applicable if an entity enters into only basic financial instruments.

There is a further unusual feature in relation to financial instruments accounting in FRS 102. As an accounting policy choice, an entity may apply either:

- sections 11 and 12 in full;

- the recognition and measurement requirements of IAS 39, 'Financial instruments: Recognition and measurement' (as adopted by the EU), and the disclosure requirements of sections 11 and 12 of FRS 102; or
- the recognition and measurement requirements of IFRS 9, 'Financial instruments', and the disclosure requirements of sections 11 and 12 of FRS 102. Because IFRS 9 would be applied via FRS 102, the FRC has noted that EU endorsement is not relevant.

The July 2015 amendments to FRS 102 include a revision to clarify that, where IFRS 9 has been applied as described above and that standard requires a financial instrument to be measured at fair value through profit or loss, such measurement must be permitted by company law; otherwise, measurement reverts back to amortised cost.

IFRS 7, 'Financial instruments: Disclosures', is not applicable to entities applying FRS 102 under any of the options. Entities that use option (b) or (c) should refer to the FRS 102 column in the tables below.

The IFRS commentary is based on the financial instruments guidance in IAS 32 and IAS 39 as well as the content in IFRS 9, 'Financial instruments'.

Financial instruments: general information

	Old UK GAAP	New UK GAAP (FRS 102)	IFRS
Accounting policy option			
	All entities apply FRS 25 to determine classification of debt and equity. FRS 26 is applicable to all entities that are either listed or prepare their financial statements in accordance with the fair value rules set out in company law. All other entities can choose to continue with non-fair value old UK GAAP (FRS 4) or apply FRS 26.	An entity has a choice of applying either: a. sections 11 and 12 of FRS 102 in full; b. the recognition and measurement requirements of IAS 39 and disclosure requirements of FRS 102 (sections 11 and 12) and the presentation requirements of paragraphs 11.38A or 12.25B of FRS 102 in relation to offsetting; or c. the recognition and measurement requirements of IFRS 9 (subject to company law requirements) and the disclosure requirements of FRS 102 (sections 11 and 12) and the presentation requirements of paragraphs 11.38A or 12.25B of FRS 102 in relation to offsetting. [FRS 102 para 11.2].	IAS 32 and IAS 39 apply to all entities. IFRS 9 has not been endorsed by the EU at the time of writing, and so it can only be applied in countries outside the EU.
Definition, scope and examples			
Definition of financial instrument	A financial instrument is any contract that gives rise to a financial asset of one entity and a financial liability or equity instrument of another entity. [FRS 25 para 11].	Same as old UK GAAP. [FRS 102 para 11.3, Glossary].	Same as FRS 102 and old UK GAAP. [IAS 32 para 11].

	Old UK GAAP	New UK GAAP (FRS 102)	IFRS

Classification as a liability	A financial liability is any liability that is:
	• a contractual obligation:
	  • to deliver cash or another financial asset to another entity; or
	  • to exchange financial assets or financial liabilities with another entity under conditions that are potentially unfavourable to the entity; or
	• a contract that will or may be settled in the entity's own equity instruments and is:
	  • a non-derivative for which the entity is or may be obliged to deliver a variable number of the entity's own equity instruments; or
	  • a derivative that will or may be settled other than by the exchange of a fixed amount of cash or another financial asset for a fixed number of the entity's own equity instruments. For this purpose, the entity's own equity instruments do not include instruments that are themselves contracts for the future receipt or delivery of the entity's own equity instruments.
	
	Certain puttable instruments are classified as equity, provided they meet certain criteria. [FRS 25 para 11].
		Similar to old UK GAAP. There is less guidance on the exemption for puttable instruments. [FRS 102 Glossary].	Same as old UK GAAP. [IAS 32 para 11].

Classification as equity	An equity instrument is any contract that evidences a residual interest in the assets of an entity after deducting all of its liabilities. [FRS 25 para 11].	Same as old UK GAAP. [FRS 102 Glossary].	Same as FRS 102 and old UK GAAP. [IAS 32 para 11].
Compound financial instruments	The issuer of a non-derivative financial instrument evaluates the terms of the financial instrument to determine whether it contains both a liability and an equity component. Each component is classified separately as a financial liability, financial asset or equity instrument. [FRS 25 para 28]. An issuer of a compound financial instrument first determines the carrying amount of the liability	Same as old UK GAAP. [FRS 102 para 22.13].	Same as FRS 102 and old UK GAAP. [IAS 32 paras 29, 32].

	Old UK GAAP	New UK GAAP (FRS 102)	IFRS
	component by measuring the fair value of a similar liability (including any embedded non-equity derivative features) that does not have an associated equity component; the equity component is then determined by deducting the fair value of the financial liability from the fair value of the compound financial instrument as a whole. [FRS 25 para 32].		
Scope	FRS 26 applies to: • any listed entity; or • an entity that applies the fair value accounting rules set out in company law. [FRS 26 para 1A]. FRS 25 and FRS 26 apply to all financial instruments, except for the following: • interests in subsidiary, quasi-subsidiary and associate undertakings, partnerships and joint ventures; • employee benefit plans; • contracts for contingent consideration in a business combination (acquirer); • insurance contracts; • financial instruments issued with a discretionary participation feature; • share-based payment transactions, unless they can be net settled; • leases; • financial instruments issued by the entity that meet the definition of an equity instrument in FRS 25; • contracts between an acquirer and a vendor in a business combination to buy or sell an acquiree at a future date; • certain loan commitments; and • reimbursement assets. [FRS 25 para 4; FRS 26 para 2].	For those applying sections 11 and 12 scope is similar to FRS 26 except for: • leases that could result in a loss to the lessor or lessee as a result of non-typical contractual terms are in the scope of section 12; • all loan commitments are in the scope of either section 11 or 12; and • financial guarantee contracts are outside the scope of sections 11 and 12, and are accounted for instead as a provision under section 21. [FRS 102 paras 11.7, 12.3]. For those applying IAS 39/IFRS 9, the scope is the same as full IFRS.	Similar to FRS 26; however, IFRS does not exclude contracts for contingent consideration in a business combination (acquirer) from its scope. [IAS 32 para 4; IAS 39 paras 2, 4; IFRS 7 para 3; IFRS 9 para 2.1].

	Old UK GAAP	New UK GAAP (FRS 102)	IFRS
	Entities not covered by FRS 26 apply FRS 4, 'Capital instruments', and the disclosure requirements of FRS 13 (if applicable).		
Categories	FRS 26 distinguishes four measurement categories of financial instruments: • financial assets or financial liabilities at fair value through profit or loss; • held-to-maturity investments; • loans and receivables; • available-for-sale financial assets; and • financial liabilities other than those at fair value through profit or loss. [FRS 26 paras 9, 45]. Not applicable to non-FRS 26 reporters.	FRS 102 distinguishes between basic and other financial instruments. Section 11 establishes measurement and reporting requirements for basic financial instruments; section 12 addresses the requirements for other financial instruments. [FRS 102 paras 11.1, 12.1].	Same as FRS 26. [IAS 39 para 9]. Under IFRS 9, financial assets are classified based on the business model of the entity and the contractual cash flow characteristics of the instrument as either: • at amortised cost; or • at fair value. Financial liabilities are classified similarly to FRS 26 and IAS 39 as: • at amortised cost; or • at fair value through profit or loss.
Examples of basic and complex financial instruments	Not applicable.	Examples of financial instruments that normally qualify as 'basic' are: • cash and demand deposits (for example, bank accounts); • trade accounts and notes receivable and payable; • loans from banks or other third parties; • commercial paper and commercial bills held; and • bonds and similar debt instruments (both held and issued). Examples of financial instruments that do not normally qualify as 'basic' are: • asset-backed securities and repurchase agreements; • options, rights, warrants, futures, forward contracts and interest rate swaps that can be settled in cash or by exchanging another financial instrument; • hedging instruments;	Not applicable.

	Old UK GAAP	New UK GAAP (FRS 102)	IFRS
		• commitments to make or receive a loan to/from another entity if that commitment can be settled net in cash; • investments in another entity's equity instruments other than non-convertible preference shares and non-puttable ordinary or preference shares; and • investments in convertible debt. [FRS 102 paras 11.5-11.6].	
Initial recognition			
	An entity recognises a financial instrument when the entity becomes a party to the contractual provisions of the instrument. Regular-way purchases or sales of financial assets are recognised using either trade date or settlement date accounting. [FRS 26 paras 14, 38]. No explicit guidance for non-FRS 26 reporters.	Same as old UK GAAP, except that there is no mention of regular-way purchases or sales. [FRS 102 paras 11.12, 12.6].	Same as old UK GAAP. [IAS 39 paras 14, 38; IFRS 9 para 3.1.1].

Basic financial instruments

	Old UK GAAP	New UK GAAP (FRS 102)	IFRS
Definition			
Basic financial instruments	Not applicable.	The following instruments are accounted for as basic financial instruments: • Cash. • Debt instruments that provide contractual returns to the holder in the same currency as the debt instrument that meet the following conditions would be accounted for as basic financial instruments. The contractual returns of the debt instrument are either a fixed amount, a positive fixed, or a positive variable rate, or a combination of a positive or a negative fixed rate and a positive variable rate (for example, LIBOR plus 200 basis points or LIBOR less 50 basis points, but not 500 basis points less LIBOR).	Not applicable.

	Old UK GAAP	New UK GAAP (FRS 102)	IFRS
		The contractual terms may provide for repayments of the principal or the return to the holder (but not both) to be linked to a single relevant observable index of general price inflation of the currency in which the debt instrument is denominated, provided such links are not leveraged. The contractual terms may provide for a determinable variation of the return to the holder during the life of instrument, provided that the new rate of return meets the basic instrument return criteria and the variation is not contingent on future events other than; a change of a contractual variable rate; to protect the holder against credit deterioration to the issuer, or to protect the holder or issuer against changes in levies applied by a central bank or taxation or law. The contractual returns do not contain provisions that could result in the holder losing principal or interest, pre-payment or put provisions contingent on future events (other than to protect the holder against credit deterioration of the issuer, change in control of the issuer, or to protect the holder or issuer against changes in levies applied by a central bank or taxation or law). Contractual provisions may permit the extension of the term of the debt instrument, provided that the return to the holder and any other contractual provision applicable during the extended term satisfy the above conditions. • A commitment to receive a loan that cannot be settled in cash and, when executed, meets the criteria of a basic instrument. • Investments in non-convertible preference shares and non-puttable ordinary shares or preference shares. [FRS 102 paras 11.8-11.9].	

	Old UK GAAP	New UK GAAP (FRS 102)	IFRS
Measurement			
Initial measurement	For a FRS 26 reporter, when a financial asset or financial liability is recognised initially, an entity measures it at its fair value plus (in the case of a financial asset or financial liability not at fair value through profit or loss) transaction costs that are directly attributable to the acquisition or issue of the financial asset or financial liability. [FRS 26 paras 43, AG64-AG65]. The fair value of a financial instrument on initial recognition is normally the transaction price. [FRS 26 paras 43, AG64]. Where an entity has an obligation to purchase its own shares for cash or another financial asset, it should recognise a liability at the present value of the redemption amount, even if the contract is an equity instrument itself. [FRS 25 para 23]. For a non-FRS 26 reporter, debt is stated immediately after issue at the amount of the net proceeds. The issue costs are accounted for as a reduction in the proceeds. [FRS 4 paras 27, 92]. For a non-FRS 26 adopter, under the Companies Act's historical cost accounting rules, fixed asset investments are recognised in the financial statements at their purchase price. Under the Act's alternative accounting rules, fixed asset investments can be included in the balance sheet either: • at their market value, determined as at the date of their last valuation; or • at a value determined on any basis that appears to the directors to be appropriate in the company's circumstances. [Company law].[1] [1] In the following, the alternative accounting rules under company law for non-FRS 26 reporters are not further considered.	Initial measurement of financial assets and liabilities is at the transaction price (including transaction costs, except for instruments at fair value through profit or loss), unless the arrangement constitutes, in effect, a financing transaction, in which case it is measured at the net present value of future payments. [FRS 102 para 11.13].	Same as FRS 26 reporters. [IAS 39 paras 43, AG64-65; IFRS 9 para 5.1.1].

	Old UK GAAP	New UK GAAP (FRS 102)	IFRS
Subsequent measurement	For a FRS 26 reporter: • Financial instruments classified as held for trading, or designated as at fair value through profit or loss, are measured at fair value through profit or loss. • Held-to-maturity investments and loans and receivables are measured at amortised cost. • Financial liabilities other than those at fair value through profit or loss are measured at amortised cost. • Available-for-sale investments are measured at fair value, with changes in fair value recorded in equity. • Investments in unquoted equity securities whose fair value cannot be measured reliably are measured at cost less impairment. [FRS 26 paras 46, 47, 66]. For a non-FRS 26 reporter, finance costs of debt are charged in the profit and loss account and allocated to periods over the term of the instrument at a constant rate on the carrying amount. Finance costs are defined as 'the difference between the net proceeds of an instrument and the total amount of the payments (or other transfers of economic benefits) that the issuer may be required to make in respect of the instrument'. [FRS 4 paras 8, 28].	At the end of each reporting period, basic debt instruments are measured at amortised cost using the effective interest method, unless designated on initial recognition at fair value through profit or loss to eliminate an accounting mismatch, or because the instrument is managed on a fair value basis. Commitments to receive or make a loan to another entity are measured at cost less impairment. Investments in non-convertible preference shares and non-puttable ordinary shares or preference shares are measured at fair value through profit or loss if fair value can be measured reliably; otherwise, at cost less impairment. [FRS 102 para 11.14].	Same as FRS 26 reporters. [IAS 39 para 9]. Under IFRS 9, where the business model is to hold financial assets to collect contractual cash flows, and those cash flows are solely payments of principal and interest, the asset will be measured at amortised cost using the effective interest method. All other financial assets are measured at fair value through profit or loss (with an option, for equity instruments which are not held for trading and is also not contingent consideration of an acquirer in a business combination to which IFRS 3 applies to present gains and losses in other comprehensive income). There is no longer an exemption from fair value measurement of unquoted equity instruments whose fair value cannot be reliably measured. Fair value is required to be estimated by using a valuation technique. Financial liabilities are measured at amortised cost, unless designated as at fair value through profit or loss, and fair value changes in credit risk are presented in other comprehensive income. [IFRS 9 paras 5.2.1, 4.2.1-4.2.2, 5.7.5].
Amortised cost	The amortised cost of a financial asset or financial liability is: • the amount at which the financial asset or financial liability is measured at initial recognition; • minus principal repayments; • plus or minus the cumulative amortisation using the effective interest method of any	Same as FRS 26 reporters. [FRS 102 para 11.15].	Same as FRS 102 and FRS 26 reporters. [IAS 39 para 9; IFRS 9 para 5.2.1].

	Old UK GAAP	New UK GAAP (FRS 102)	IFRS
	difference between that initial amount and the maturity amount; and • minus any reduction (directly or through the use of an allowance account) for impairment or uncollectibility. [FRS 26 para 9]. For a non-FRS 26 reporter, finance costs of debt and non-equity shares are charged in the profit and loss account, and allocated to periods over the term of the instrument at a constant rate on the carrying amount. The carrying amount of debt is increased by the finance cost in respect of the reporting period and reduced by payments made in respect of the debt in that period. [FRS 4 paras 28-29].		
Effective interest method	An FRS 26 reporter uses the effective interest method of calculating the amortised cost of a financial asset or a financial liability and allocates the interest income or interest expense over the relevant period. [FRS 26 para 9]. For a non-FRS 26 reporter, finance costs of debt are charged in the profit and loss account and allocated to periods over the term of the instrument at a constant rate on the carrying amount. [FRS 4 para 28].	Same as FRS 26 reporters. [FRS 102 para 11.16].	Same as FRS 26 reporters and FRS 102. [IAS 39 para 9; IFRS 9 para 5.2.1].
Fair value – investments in ordinary or preference shares	For an FRS 26 reporter, the best evidence of fair value is quoted prices in an active market. If the market for a financial instrument is not active, an entity establishes fair value by using a valuation technique. [FRS 26 para 48A]. For the entities not covered by FRS 26, measurement of financial instruments at fair value is not relevant.	Similar to FRS 26 reporters. In some circumstances, prices for recent transactions may be used. The best evidence of a fair value is a quoted price in an active market. [FRS 102 para 11.27].	Fair value is the price that would be received to sell an asset in an orderly transaction in the principal (or most advantageous) market at the measurement date under current market conditions (ie an exit price) regardless of whether that price is directly observable or estimated using a valuation technique. [IFRS 13 para 24].

	Old UK GAAP	New UK GAAP (FRS 102)	IFRS
Fair value – valuation technique	The objective of using a valuation technique is to establish what the transaction price would have been on the measurement date in an arm's length exchange motivated by normal business considerations. Valuation techniques include: • using recent arm's length market transactions between knowledgeable, willing parties, if available; • reference to the current fair value of another instrument that is substantially the same; • discounted cash flow analysis; and • option pricing models. [FRS 26 paras 48A, AG74-AG79].	Same as FRS 26 reporters, except that detailed guidance is not given. [FRS 102 paras 11.28-11.29].	IFRS 13 is effective from 1 January 2013. The fair value of all liabilities, including derivative liabilities, is determined based on the assumption that the liability will be transferred to another party (an 'exit price') rather than otherwise settled or extinguished; and for quoted financial assets and liabilities the most representative price within the bid-ask spread should be used. [IFRS 13 paras 5, 34, 70].
Fair value – no active market for equity instruments	The fair value of investments in equity instruments that do not have a quoted market price in an active market (and derivatives that are linked to, and must be settled by delivery of, such an unquoted equity instrument) is reliably measurable if: • the variability in the range of reasonable fair value estimates is not significant for that instrument; or • the probabilities of the various estimates within the range can be reasonably assessed and used in estimating fair value. If the range of reasonable fair value estimates is significant, and the probabilities of the various estimates cannot be reasonably assessed, an entity is precluded from measuring the instrument at fair value. [FRS 26 paras AG80-AG81].	Similar to FRS 26 reporters, except that FRS 102 explicitly states that, if a reliable measure of fair values for an asset is no longer available, the carrying value at the last date the asset was reliably measurable becomes its cost. [FRS 102 paras 11.30-11.32].	IFRS 13 fair value measurement guidance is used to determine fair value. Under IFRS 9, there is no exemption from fair value measurement of equity instruments that do not have a quoted market price in an active market. A valuation technique is required to be applied, although (in limited cases) cost may represent the best estimate of fair value. [IFRS 9 para B5.4.14].
Impairment of financial instruments not measured at fair value through profit or loss			
General	For FRS 26 reporters, an entity assesses at each balance sheet date whether there is any objective evidence that a financial asset or group of financial assets is impaired (the 'incurred loss' method). Impairment losses are recognised in profit or loss.	For assets measured at cost or amortised cost, similar to FRS 26 reporters; however, less detailed guidance is given, and all impairment losses are reversed in profit or loss if there is objective evidence of the reversal. [FRS 102 paras 11.21, 11.26].	Same as FRS 26 reporters. [IAS 39 paras 58, 63, 66, 69]. IFRS 9 adopts a 'three-stage' model for impairment based on changes in credit quality since initial recognition and is measured using an 'expected credit loss' approach.

	Old UK GAAP	New UK GAAP (FRS 102)	IFRS
	Impairment tests are performed for financial assets carried at cost, for financial assets carried at amortised cost, and for available-for-sale financial assets. Impairment losses on equity instruments carried at cost or available-for-sale equity instruments are not reversed. [FRS 26 paras 58, 63, 66, 69]. For non FRS 26 reporters, the requirements of FRS 11, 'Impairment', are applied for investments in subsidiaries, associates and joint ventures. See 'Impairment of assets'. For other fixed asset investments, under the Companies Act, permanent diminutions in value must be recognised in the profit and loss account, and temporary diminutions in value may be charged to the profit and loss account. [SI 2008/410 1 Sch 19]. Current asset investments should be measured at the lower of cost and net realisable value; and any fall below cost should be recognised in the profit and loss account. [SI 2008/410 1 Sch 23, 24].		
Assets measured at amortised cost	For FRS 26 reporters, any impairment loss is measured as the difference between the asset's carrying amount and the present value of estimated future cash flows (excluding future credit losses that have not been incurred) discounted at the financial asset's original effective interest rate. [FRS 26 para 63].	Similar to FRS 26 reporters, except less detailed guidance is given. [FRS 102 para 11.25(a)].	Same as FRS 26 reporters. [IAS 39 para 63]. IFRS 9 adopts a 'three-stage' model for impairment based on changes in credit quality since initial recognition and is measured using an 'expected credit loss' approach.
Assets measured at cost	For FRS 26 reporters, any impairment loss is measured as the difference between the carrying amount of the financial asset and the present value of estimated future cash flows discounted at the current market rate of return for a similar financial asset. [FRS 26 para 66].	For an instrument measured at cost less impairment, the impairment loss is the difference between the asset's carrying amount and the best estimate of the amount that the entity would receive for the asset if it were to be sold. [FRS 102 para 11.25(b)].	Same as FRS 26 reporters. [IAS 39 para 66]. Under IFRS 9 equity instruments are measured at fair value. [IFRS 9 paras 4.1.1-4.1.2].

	Old UK GAAP	New UK GAAP (FRS 102)	IFRS
Derecognition			

Financial assets	For FRS 26 reporters, an entity derecognises a financial asset only when:
	• the contractual rights to the cash flows from the financial asset expire; or
	• it transfers the financial asset (either by transferring the contractual right to the cash flows or by meeting certain 'pass through' requirements); and
	  • transfers substantially all the risks and rewards of ownership; or
	  • neither transfers nor retains substantially all risks and rewards of ownership, but does not retain control of the asset.
	Where an entity transfers a financial asset, and neither transfers or retains substantially all risks of the asset, but retains control, it continues to recognise the asset to the extent of its continuing involvement. [FRS 26 paras 17-37].
	For non-FRS 26 reporters, the general derecognition criteria in FRS 5 apply for transactions in previously recognised assets:
	• An asset should cease to be recognised in its entirety, or part, only where there is a significant change in the entity's rights to benefits and exposure to risks.
	• Linked presentation applies for certain non-recourse finance arrangements.
		Similar to FRS 26 reporters, but without the 'pass through' requirements or continuing involvement concept for transferred assets. Hence, an entity only derecognises a financial asset when:
		• the contractual rights to the cash flows from the asset have expired or are settled;
		• the entity has transferred substantially all the risks and rewards of ownership of the financial asset; or
		• the entity has retained some significant risks and rewards, but has transferred control of the asset to another party. In this case, the asset is derecognised, and any rights and obligations created or retained are recognised. [FRS 102 para 11.33].
			Same as FRS 26 reporters. [IAS 39 paras 17-37; IFRS 9 paras 3.2.1-3.2.9].

Financial liabilities	For FRS 26 reporters, a financial liability (or a part of a financial liability) is removed from the balance sheet only when it is extinguished – that is, when the obligation specified in the contract is discharged, cancelled or expires. [FRS 26 para 39].	Financial liabilities are derecognised only when they are extinguished – that is, when the obligation is discharged, cancelled or expires. [FRS 102 para 11.36].	Same as FRS 26 reporters. [IAS 39 para 39; IFRS 9 para 3.3.1].

	Old UK GAAP	New UK GAAP (FRS 102)	IFRS
	For FRS 26 reporters, if an existing borrower and lender exchange financial instruments with substantially different terms, the entities account for the transaction as an extinguishment of the original financial liability and the recognition of a new financial liability. For non-FRS 26 reporters, there are no specific derecognition criteria.	Same as FRS 26 although less guidance on the meaning of 'substantially different'. [FRS 102 paras 11.37-11.38].	Same as FRS 26 reporters. [IAS 39 paras 40–41; IFRS 9 paras 3.3.2-3.3.3].
	The entity recognises in profit or loss any difference between the carrying amount of the liability extinguished or transferred and the consideration paid, including any non-cash assets transferred or liabilities assumed. [FRS 26 paras 40-41].	Same.	Same.
	If a financial liability is settled through the issuance of the entity's own equity instruments, a gain or loss is recognised in profit or loss, being the difference in the carrying value of the liability and the fair value of the equity issued. [UITF 47]. For non-FRS 26 reporters, there are no specific criteria.	Not addressed by FRS 102.	Same as FRS 26 reporters. [IFRIC 19].

Other financial instruments

	Old UK GAAP	New UK GAAP (FRS 102)	IFRS
Definition			
Other financial instruments	Classification basis different. See categories section under basic financial instruments above.	Other financial instruments are all financial instruments, except basic financial instruments (covered by section 11). Section 12 applies to all contracts to buy or sell non-financial items (such as commodities, inventory or property, plant and equipment) that impose risk on the buyer or seller that are not typical of contracts to buy or sell non-financial items – for example, they are unrelated to changes in price of the non-financial item, foreign exchange or default. [FRS 102 para 12.4]. Section 12 also applies to contracts to buy or sell non-financial items that can be settled net in cash	Classification basis different. See categories section under basic financial instruments above.

	Old UK GAAP	New UK GAAP (FRS 102)	IFRS
		or another financial instrument or by exchanging financial instruments, except for contracts entered into and held for the purpose of receipt or delivery of a non-financial item. [FRS 102 para 12.5].	
Measurement			
Initial measurement	For FRS 26 reporters, when a financial asset or financial liability is recognised initially, an entity measures it at its fair value plus (in the case of a financial asset or financial liability not at fair value through profit or loss) transaction costs that are directly attributable to the acquisition or issue of the financial asset or financial liability. The fair value of a financial instrument on initial recognition is normally the transaction price. [FRS 26; FRS 43 para AG64]. For non-FRS 26 reporters, there is no specific guidance for accounting for derivatives or similarly complex financial instruments. They are typically held at cost (often nil for derivatives) and are therefore 'off balance sheet' and only accounted for if they satisfy the definition of an onerous contract under FRS 12. Certain entities that enter into speculative financial contracts may consider it more appropriate to adopt a mark-to-market accounting policy.	Same as FRS 26 reporters. At initial recognition, financial assets and financial liabilities are measured at their fair value. This is normally the transaction price. [FRS 102 para 12.7].	Same as FRS 26 reporters. [IAS 39 paras 43, AG64–AG65; IFRS 9 para 5.1.1].
Subsequent measurement	For FRS 26 reporters: • Financial instruments classified as held for trading, or designated as at fair value through profit or loss, are measured at fair value through profit or loss. • Held-to-maturity investments and loans and receivables are measured at amortised cost. • Financial liabilities other than those at fair value through profit or loss are measured at amortised cost.	At the end of each reporting period, financial instruments are measured at fair value through profit or loss, except for: 1. Equity instruments that are not publicly traded and whose fair value cannot otherwise be measured reliably; and contracts linked to such instruments that, if exercised, will result in delivery of such instruments. These are measured at cost less impairment. Cost is defined as fair value on the last date it was reliably measurable.	Same as FRS 26 reporters. [IAS 39 paras 46-47, 66]. Under IFRS 9, there is no longer an exemption from fair value measurement of unquoted equity instruments whose fair value cannot be reliably measured. A valuation technique is required to be applied. Where the business model is to hold financial assets to collect contractual cash flows, and those cash flows are solely payments of principal and interest, the asset will be measured at amortised

	Old UK GAAP	New UK GAAP (FRS 102)	IFRS
	• Available-for-sale investments are measured at fair value, with changes in fair value recorded in other comprehensive income. • Investments in equity securities whose fair value cannot be measured reliably are measured at cost less impairment. [FRS 26 paras 46–47].	2. Hedging instruments in a designated hedging relationship. 3. Financial instruments that are not permitted by company law to be measured at fair value through profit and loss shall be measured at amortised cost. [FRS 102 paras 12.8-12.9].	cost using the effective interest method. All other financial assets are measured at fair value through profit or loss (with an option for equity instruments which are not held for trading and is also not contingent consideration of an acquirer in a business combination to which IFRS 3 applies to present this in other comprehensive income). Financial liabilities are measured at amortised cost unless designated as at fair value through profit or loss, with fair value changes in credit risk presented in other comprehensive income. [IFRS 9 paras 5.2.1, 4.2.1-4.2.2].
Hedge accounting			
General	FRS 26 reporters may designate a hedging relationship between a hedging instrument and a hedged item that qualify for hedge accounting if certain criteria are met. [FRS 26 para 71]. For non-FRS 26 reporters, there are no specified criteria for hedge accounting. SSAP 20.6 considers the use of forward contracts; SSAP 20.27-20.32 consider hedging foreign currency equity investments.	An entity may designate a hedging relationship between a hedging instrument and a hedged item that qualify for hedge accounting if certain criteria are met. [FRS 102 para 12.15]. FRS 102 permits hedge accounting where there is an *economic relationship* between the hedged item and hedging instrument (subject to certain other conditions being met, detailed below), with the result that a wider range of hedges will qualify for hedge accounting than under FRS 26.	Same as FRS 26 reporters. [IAS 39 para 71]. IFRS 9 is similar to new UK GAAP. [IFRS 9 para 6.1.1 and 6.4.1].
Criteria for hedge accounting	For FRS 26 reporters, a hedging relationship qualifies for hedge accounting only if all of the following conditions are met: • at the inception of the hedge, there is formal designation and documentation of the hedging relationship and the entity's risk management objective and strategy for undertaking the hedge; • the hedge is expected to be highly effective; • for cash flow hedges, a forecast transaction that is the subject of the hedge must be highly probable and must present an exposure to	In order to apply hedge accounting, management prepares documentation at the inception of the relationship. This documentation clearly identifies the risk being hedged, the hedging instrument, the hedged item and causes of hedge ineffectiveness. A range of risks, hedged items and hedging instruments are permitted, as described in more detail below. In addition, there must be an economic relationship between the hedged item and hedging instrument in order to apply hedge accounting. [FRS 102 para 12.18].	Same as FRS 26 reporters. [IAS 39 para 88]. IFRS 9 is similar to new UK GAAP. In addition the entity must document the risk management objective and strategy for undertaking the hedge and how it will assess whether the hedge effectiveness requirements (for example, economic relationship and appropriate hedge ratio) are met. [IFRS 9 para 6.4.1].

	Old UK GAAP	New UK GAAP (FRS 102)	IFRS
	variations in cash flows that could ultimately affect profit or loss; • the effectiveness of the hedge can be reliably measured; and • the hedge is assessed on an ongoing basis. [FRS 26 para 88].		
Risks for which hedge accounting is permitted	FRS 26 permits three types of hedging relationship: • Cash flow hedges. • Fair value hedges. • Hedges of a net investment in a foreign operation. [FRS 26 para 86]. A broad array of risks is eligible for hedging under FRS 26 (for example, equity price risk and one-sided risks).	Similar to FRS 26 reporters. [FRS 102 para 12.19].	Same as old UK GAAP for FRS 26 reporters. [IAS 39 paras 86, AG99F]. IFRS 9 is similar to FRS 26 and FRS 102. [IFRS 9 para 6.5.2]. Details of the main differences are provided below.
	FRS 26 allows a group of similar items to be designated as a hedged item. [FRS 26 para AG99F].	Same as FRS 26 – it does not include items with offsetting risk positions. [FRS 102 para 12.16B].	IFRS 9 allows a group of items to be designated as a hedged item. This includes allowing both an aggregated exposure which may include a derivative or a group of items with offsetting (net) risk positions to be designated as the hedged item in certain cases. [IFRS 9 paras 6.3.4 and 6.6.1].
	FRS 26 restricts the risks or portions of a financial instrument that can be designated as the hedged item, based on the principle that those risks or portions must be separately identifiable and reliably measurable. FRS 26 does not allow any risks or portions of a non-financial item to be designated as a hedged item (with the exception of foreign currency risk). [FRS 26 para 82, AG 100].	Unlike FRS 26, FRS 102 allows components of both financial and non-financial items to be designated as the hedged item, as long as those risks or portions are separately identifiable and reliably measurable. [FRS 102 para 12.16C].	Like FRS 102, IFRS 9 allows components of both financial and non-financial items to be designated as the hedged item, as long as those components are separately identifiable and reliably measurable but provides more guidance than new UK GAAP on how this may be applied in practice. [IFRS 9 para 6.3.1-7 and 6.6.1-3].
Hedging instruments for which hedge accounting is permitted	FRS 26 permits hedging instruments to be: • derivatives that are not net written options; and • non-derivative assets or liabilities used as a hedge of foreign currency risk.	Similar to FRS 26 reporters. [FRS 102 paras 12.17 and 12.17A-C].	Same as FRS 26 reporters. [IAS 39 paras 82-88]. IFRS 9 is similar to FRS 26 reporters. [IFRS 9 para 6.2.4-6].

	Old UK GAAP	New UK GAAP (FRS 102)	IFRS
	FRS 26 requires that the hedging instrument involves a party external to the reporting entity. Features of a hedging instrument, such as pre-payment, early termination or extensions, do not restrict the use of hedge accounting, provided the entity can demonstrate that the hedge is highly effective. FRS 26 allows groups of derivatives (or a non-derivative and derivative) to be designated as a combined hedging instrument in certain cases. FRS 26 allows a single hedging instrument to be designated as a hedge of multiple risks. [FRS 26 paras 72-77, 82].		
	Management is permitted to separately designate the intrinsic value of an option or the spot component of a forward contract. FRS 26 therefore allows a range of hedging instruments to be used (for example, interest rate collars, purchased options and foreign currency borrowings).	However, there is no detailed guidance in FRS 102 on how to designate and account for the time value of an option and forward element or foreign currency basis spread on a forward contract.	However, the time value of an option and forward element or foreign currency basis spread on a forward contract may be accounted for as a 'cost of hedging' under IFRS 9.
Effectiveness testing	The entity is required to perform quantitative retrospective and prospective effectiveness tests at least at each reporting date. In order to apply hedge accounting, the retrospective test must demonstrate that the actual results of the hedge are within a range of 80%-125%. A specific method for testing effectiveness is not defined, but the entity documents its chosen method as part of the hedge documentation. [FRS 26 para 88].	FRS 102 does not require quantitative assessments of hedge effectiveness but entities must discontinue the hedge if they no longer meet the conditions for hedge accounting. [FRS 102 para 12.25].	Same as FRS 26 reporters. [IAS 39 para 88]. IFRS 9 reporters must continue to meet the qualifying criteria in para 6.4.1, in particular to be able to demonstrate prospectively at each reporting date that there is an economic relationship between the hedged item and hedging instrument. There is no retrospective effectiveness test under IFRS 9 but ineffectiveness must be recorded in profit or loss. [IFRS 9 paras 6.4.1, 6.5.8(a) and 6.5.11(c)].

	Old UK GAAP	New UK GAAP (FRS 102)	IFRS
Cash flow hedges – hedges of variable interest rate risk or foreign exchange risk of a recognised financial instrument, foreign exchange risk or interest rate risk in a firm commitment or highly probable forecast transaction or commodity price risk in a highly probable forecast transaction, or foreign exchange risk in a net investment in a foreign operation	The portion of the gain or loss on the hedging instrument that is determined to be an effective hedge is recognised through the statement of total recognised gains and losses. The ineffective portion is recognised in profit or loss – the ineffective portion is the excess (if any) of the cumulative change in fair value of the hedging instrument over the cumulative change in the fair value of the expected cash flows.	Same as FRS 26 reporters, except that movements are recognised through other comprehensive income not through the statement of recognised gains and losses. [FRS 102 para 12.23].	Same as new UK GAAP under IAS 39 and IFRS 9.
	Hedge accounting is discontinued when: • the hedging instrument expires, is sold, terminated or exercised; • the hedge no longer meets the criteria for hedge accounting; • the forecast transaction is no longer highly probable; or • the entity revokes the designation. [FRS 26 paras 95-101].	Same as FRS 26 reporters [FRS 102 para 12.25].	Same as FRS 26 reporters. [IAS 39 paras 95-101]. IFRS 9 is similar to FRS 26 and new UK GAAP, except that IFRS 9 does not permit voluntary de-designation of a hedge if the hedging objective and all other criteria are still met. Instead, IFRS 9 requires mandatory rebalancing of the hedge ratio. [IFRS 9 paras 6.5.5 and Appendix B para B6.5.23].
	The amount recognised in the statement of total recognised gains and losses is recognised in profit or loss when the hedged item affects profit or loss or when the hedging relationship ends. [FRS 26 para 100].	The amount recognised in other comprehensive income is recognised in profit or loss when the hedged item affects profit or loss or when the hedging relationship ends, except for exchange differences that relate to a hedge of a net investment in a foreign operation which are not recycled. [FRS 102 para 12.25A].	Same as FRS 26 reporters. [IAS 39 para 100]. IFRS 9 is similar to FRS 26 and new UK GAAP, except that exchange differences that relate to a hedge of a net investment in a foreign operation are recycled (unlike new UK GAAP) and a basis adjustment is required for hedges of forecast transactions that result in recognition of a non-financial asset or liability on balance sheet (optional under IAS 39 and FRS 26). [IFRS 9 para 6.5.11(d)].
	The amounts that were recognised in the statement of total recognised gains and losses prior to discontinuance of the hedge are recognised in profit or loss when the hedged item is derecognised or when a forecast transaction is no longer expected to take place. [FRS 26 para 101].	Same as FRS 26 reporters, except that the original amounts were recognised through other comprehensive income not through the statement of recognised gains and losses. [FRS 102 para 12.23(d)].	Same as new UK GAAP under IAS 39 and IFRS 9.

	Old UK GAAP	New UK GAAP (FRS 102)	IFRS
Fair value hedges – hedges of fixed interest rate risk or foreign exchange risk of a recognised financial instrument or commodity price risk in a firm commitment or of a commodity held	The hedged item is adjusted for the gain or loss attributable to the hedged risk. That element is included in profit or loss to offset the impact of the hedging instrument.	Same as FRS 26 reporters	Same as FRS 26 reporters under IAS 39 and IFRS 9. [IAS 39 paras 89-94]. [IFRS 9 para 6.5.8].
	An entity discontinues prospectively the hedge accounting if: • the hedging instrument expires or is sold, terminated or exercised; • the hedge no longer meets the criteria for hedge accounting; or • the entity revokes the designation. [FRS 26 paras 89, 91].	Same as FRS 26 reporters. [FRS 102 paras 12.25].	Same as FRS 26 reporters. [IAS 39 paras 95-101]. Similar to FRS 26 and new UK GAAP, except that IFRS 9 does not permit voluntary de-designation of a hedge if the hedging objective and all other criteria are still met. Instead, IFRS 9 requires mandatory rebalancing of the hedge ratio. [IFRS 9 paras 6.5.5 and Appendix B para B6.5.23].
	On discontinuance of a hedge of an asset or liability measured at amortised cost, the adjustment previously made to the hedged item is amortised to profit or loss using the effective interest method. [FRS 26 para 92].	Same as FRS 26 reporters. [FRS 102 para 12.22].	Same as FRS 26 reporters under IAS 39 and IFRS 9. [IAS 39 paras 89-94]. [IFRS 9 para 6.5.10].

Disclosure of financial instruments

Disclosures	FRS 26 reporters (but excluding most subsidiaries) must give FRS 29 disclosures about: • categories of financial instruments, carrying amounts and impact on profit or loss; • derecognition; • collateral; • accounting policies; • hedge accounting; • fair value, including analysing instruments into the fair value hierarchy (levels 1, 2 and 3) based on the reliability of valuations; and • nature and extent of risks (narrative and quantitative disclosures of credit, liquidity and market risk).	All entities must give the disclosures required by the Companies Act. For qualifying entities (that is, most subsidiaries) that are not financial institutions, there is exemption from some the disclosures in sections 11 and 12 of FRS 102. For entities that are not qualifying entities or financial institutions, the disclosures in sections 11 and 12 of FRS 102 must be given. These are similar to the FRS 29 requirements, but with no additional disclosure of the extent and nature of all financial instruments or fair value hierarchy information). [FRS 102 paras 11.39-11.48A; 12.26-12.29A]. For entities that are not qualifying entities but are financial institutions or pension funds, disclosures under sections 11 and 34 of FRS 102 are required.	Similar to old UK GAAP disclosures under FRS 29, with additional capital disclosures, but greater narrative and quantitative disclosure about unobservable significant inputs for level 3 fair valuations. [IFRS 7; IAS 1 paras 134-136; IFRS 13 paras 91-99]. IFRS 7 also includes new hedging disclosures for IFRS 9 reporters. [IFRS 7 paras 21-24]. The Act's disclosures do not apply. *FRS 101 RDF (IFRS): There is an exemption from the disclosure requirements in IFRS 7 and the disclosure requirements for fair value measurement of financial instruments in IFRS 13. [FRS 101 paras 8(d),(e)]. But the exemption does not extend to financial institutions. Also, non-financial institutions that have financial instruments held at*

	Similar disclosures are required under FRS 13 for banks and similar financial institutions outside the scope of FRS 29. In addition, all entities are required to make disclosures required by the Companies Act, including: • valuation models and techniques; • fair values and amounts in profit or loss; • extent and nature of all derivatives; • transfers to and from fair value reserve [SI 2008/410 1 Sch 55]; • fair value of derivatives not at fair value [SI 2008/410 1 Sch 56]; and • reasons for not providing for financial fixed assets at cost where fair value is less [SI 2008/410 1 Sch 57]. In addition, under the Act, for certain instruments at fair value (for example, financial liabilities designated at fair value through profit or loss and investments in associates at fair value), all the disclosures in accounting standards must be given for those instruments. [SI 2008/410 1 Sch 36].	These are similar to the FRS 29 disclosures, but with additional disclosure of capital, and less disclosure of level 3 valuations. [FRS 102 paras 11.39-11.48C, 34.17-34.48].	*fair value are required to give some disclosures under company law.*

Areas covered in IFRS and old UK GAAP for FRS 26 reporters, but not in FRS 102, include:

- Embedded derivatives.
- Reclassifications between categories of financial instruments.

Further guidance on these areas is available in the Manual of accounting – IFRS.

Foreign currencies

Old UK GAAP and IFRS are the same for entities that have adopted FRS 26 and therefore use FRS 23. Other entities would continue to apply SSAP 20 under old UK GAAP.

	Old UK GAAP	New UK GAAP (FRS 102)	IFRS
Definitions			
Functional currency	FRS 23 defines functional currency as the currency of the primary economic environment in which the entity operates. [FRS 23 para 8]. SSAP 20 uses the term 'local currency', which is defined as the currency of the primary economic environment in which the entity operates and generates net cash flows. SSAP 20 does not provide any further guidance on how to determine an entity's local or functional currency. [SSAP 20 para 39].	Same as old UK GAAP for FRS 23 reporters. [FRS 102 para 30.2].	Same as old UK GAAP for FRS 23 reporters and new UK GAAP. [IAS 21 para 8].
Presentation currency	FRS 23 defines presentation currency as the currency in which the financial statements are presented. [FRS 23 para 8]. SSAP 20 does not include the concept of a presentation currency. Under SSAP 20, financial statements are prepared in the entity's 'local' currency.	Same as old UK GAAP for FRS 23 reporters. [FRS 102 Glossary].	Same as old UK GAAP for FRS 23 reporters and new UK GAAP. [IAS 21 para 8].
Functional currency			
General	All components of the financial statements are measured in the 'functional' (FRS 23) or 'local' (SSAP 20) currency. All transactions entered into in currencies other than the functional currency are treated as transactions in a foreign currency. [FRS 23 paras 17, 21; SSAP 20 paras 4, 16-17].	Same as old UK GAAP for FRS 23 reporters. [FRS 102 paras 30.6-30.7].	Same as old UK GAAP for FRS 23 reporters and new UK GAAP. [IAS 21 paras 17-21].
Foreign currency transactions	A transaction in a foreign currency is recorded in the functional (FRS 23) or local (SSAP 20) currency, using the exchange rate at the date of transaction (average rates may be used if they do not fluctuate significantly). [FRS 23 paras 21-22; SSAP 20 para 46].	Same as old UK GAAP for FRS 23 reporters. [FRS 102 paras 30.7-8].	Same as old UK GAAP for FRS 23 reporters and new UK GAAP. [IAS 21 paras 21-23].

	Old UK GAAP	New UK GAAP (FRS 102)	IFRS
	Foreign currency monetary assets and liabilities are translated at the closing rate. [FRS 23 para 23; SSAP 20 para 48]. SSAP 20 reporters may also use a contracted rate where a monetary item is to be settled at that rate. Where there are related forward contracts in respect of trading transactions, the rates of exchange specified in those contracts may be used. [SSAP 20 para 48].	At the end of each reporting period, foreign currency monetary balances are translated using the closing rate. [FRS 102 para 30.9].	Same as old UK GAAP for FRS 23 reporters and new UK GAAP. [IAS 21 para 23].
	For FRS 23 reporters, non-monetary balances denominated in a foreign currency and carried: • at cost are reported using the exchange rate at the date of the transaction; • at fair value are reported using the exchange rate at the date when the fair values were determined. [FRS 23 para 23].	Same as old UK GAAP for FRS 23 reporters. [FRS 102 para 30.9].	Same as old UK GAAP for FRS 23 reporters and new UK GAAP. [IAS 21 para 23].
	For SSAP 20 reporters, where a non-monetary item has been translated at the rate ruling when it was originally recorded, no subsequent translation of the asset is normally required. [SSAP 20 para 47].		
Recognition of exchange differences	For FRS 23 reporters, exchange differences on monetary items are recognised in profit or loss for the period. In consolidated financial statements, differences arising on a monetary item that forms part of an entity's net investment in a foreign entity (subject to strict criteria of what qualifies as net investment) are recognised initially in other comprehensive income and are reclassified from equity to profit or loss on disposal of the foreign operation. [FRS 23 paras 28, 30, 32]. For SSAP 20 reporters, exchange gains or losses on settled transactions and on unsettled monetary items are normally reported as part of the profit or loss for the year.	Same as for old UK GAAP for FRS 23 reporters, except that recycling through profit or loss of any cumulative exchange differences that were previously accumulated in equity on disposal of a foreign operation is not permitted. [FRS 102 paras 30.10, 30.12-30.13].	Same as old UK GAAP for FRS 23 reporters. [IAS 21 paras 28, 30, 32].

	Old UK GAAP	New UK GAAP (FRS 102)	IFRS
	If the conditions set out in SSAP 20 are met, exchange differences on foreign currency borrowings taken out to hedge against investments in foreign operations may be taken to reserves. [SSAP 20 para 51, 57]. Exchange differences are not recycled from the statement of total recognised gains and losses to the profit and loss account. [SSAP 20 paras 29-30, 49-50; FRS 3 para 26].	Hedge accounting requirements are dealt with in section 12.	Hedge accounting requirements are dealt with in IAS 39, IFRS 9.
Change in functional currency	For FRS 23 reporters, a change is justified only if there are changes in underlying transactions, events and conditions that are relevant to the entity. The effect of a change in functional currency is accounted for prospectively from the date of change. [FRS 23 paras 35–37]. This is not addressed in SSAP 20; however, in practice, a change in local currency is accounted for prospectively from the date of change.	Same as old UK GAAP for FRS 23 reporters. [FRS 102 paras 30.14-30.16].	Same as old UK GAAP for FRS 23 reporters and new UK GAAP. [IAS 21 paras 35-37].
Presentation currency			
General	For an FRS 23 reporter, an entity may choose to present its financial statements in any currency. If the presentation currency differs from the functional currency, an entity translates its results and financial position into the presentation currency. [FRS 23 para 38]. There is no concept of presentation currency in SSAP 20; local currency is used.	Same as old UK GAAP for FRS 23 reporters. [FRS 102 para 30.17].	Same as old UK GAAP for FRS 23 reporters and new UK GAAP. [IAS 21 para 38].
Translation to the presentation currency	For FRS 23 reporters, assets and liabilities are translated at the closing rate. Income and expenses in the statement of comprehensive income are translated using the exchange rate at the date of transaction (average rates may be used if they do not fluctuate significantly).	Same as old UK GAAP for FRS 23 reporters, except that recycling through profit or loss of any cumulative exchange differences that were previously accumulated in equity on disposal of a foreign operation is not permitted. [FRS 102 paras 30.12-30.13, 30.18-30.19].	Same as old UK GAAP for FRS 23 reporters. [IAS 21 paras 39-40, 48].
	All exchange differences are recognised initially in other comprehensive income and are reclassified from equity to profit or loss on disposal of the foreign operation. [FRS 23 paras 39, 40, 48].		

	Old UK GAAP	New UK GAAP (FRS 102)	IFRS
	There is no concept of presentation currency in SSAP 20. When preparing consolidated financial statements, the closing rate/net investment method is normally used. The assets and liabilities are translated at the closing rate at the date of the statement of financial position; income and expenses are translated using closing rate or an average rate for the period. [SSAP 20 paras 16-17, 54].		
Temporal method/functional currency of non-autonomous entity	Where a foreign entity's trade is more dependent on the economic environment of the investment company's currency than that of its own, the temporal method is used: the foreign entity's financial statements are included in the consolidation as if all the transactions have been entered into by the investing company. [SSAP 20 paras 22, 55].	There is no concept of the 'temporal method'; each entity has to determine its functional currency. A foreign entity, where trade is dependent on the economic environment of the investing company's currency, will have the same functional currency.	Same as new UK GAAP.

Hyperinflation

Old UK GAAP and IFRS are similar for entities that have adopted FRS 26 and therefore use FRS 24. Other entities would apply UITF 9 under old UK GAAP.

	Old UK GAAP	New UK GAAP (FRS 102)	IFRS
Definition	For FRS 24 users, hyperinflation is indicated by characteristics of the economic environment of a country. One of the indicators is if the cumulative inflation rate over three years is approaching, or exceeds, 100%. [FRS 24 para 3]. For UITF 9 users, adjustments are required where the cumulative inflation rate over three years is approaching, or exceeds, 100% and the operations in the hyperinflationary economies are material. [UITF 9 para 5].	Same as old UK GAAP for FRS 24 users. [FRS 102 para 31.2].	Same as old UK GAAP for FRS 24 users and new UK GAAP. [IAS 29 para 3].
Presentation	For FRS 24 users, where an entity's functional currency is the currency of a hyperinflationary economy, the financial statements are stated in terms of the measuring unit current at the balance sheet date. The gain or loss on the net monetary	Same as old UK GAAP for FRS 24 users. [FRS 102 paras 31.3, 30.13].	Same as old UK GAAP for FRS 24 users and new UK GAAP. [IAS 29 paras 8-9].

	Old UK GAAP	New UK GAAP (FRS 102)	IFRS
	position is included in profit or loss and separately disclosed. [FRS 24 paras 8-9]. For UITF 9 users, the UITF suggests two methods to deal with hyperinflationary economies in order to eliminate the distortions: • adjust the local currency financial statements to reflect current price levels before the translation process is undertaken. This includes taking any gain or loss on the net monetary position through the profit and loss account; or • use a relatively stable currency (which would not necessarily be sterling) as the functional currency (that is, the currency of measurement) for the relevant foreign operations. The functional currency would, in effect, be the 'local currency'. In such circumstances, if the transactions are not recorded initially in that stable currency, they are first remeasured into that currency. [UITF 9 para 6].		

2. Income statement and related notes

Income

Section 23 of FRS 102 (Revenue) addresses the various categories of revenue recognition (sale of goods, rendering of services, interest, royalties and dividends, construction contracts and barter transactions). Grants are addressed in section 24.

There is no separate accounting standard dealing with revenue recognition under old UK GAAP. However, Application Note G to FRS 5, 'Reporting the substance of transactions', includes guidance on revenue recognition. SSAP 9 and UITF 40 also provide guidance on revenue recognition under long-term contracts and service contracts.

	Old UK GAAP	New UK GAAP (FRS 102)	IFRS
Definitions			
Turnover/revenue	Turnover is the revenue resulting from exchange transactions under which a seller supplies to customers the goods or services that it is in the business to provide – that is, as part of its operating activities. [FRS 5 App Note G11].	'Turnover' is defined as the amounts derived from the provision of goods and services falling within the entity's ordinary activities, after deduction of: a. trade discounts; b. value added tax; and c. any other taxes based on the amounts so derived. (The July 2015 amendments to FRS 102 delete the reference to "falling within the entity's ordinary activities".) 'Revenue' is the gross inflow of economic benefits during the period arising in the course of the ordinary activities of an entity where those inflows result in increases in equity, other than increases relating to contributions from equity participants. It is referred to by a variety of names, including sales, fees, interest, dividends, royalties and rent. [FRS 102 Glossary].	IFRS does not include the term 'turnover', which is derived from UK company law. The definition of 'revenue' is the same as new UK GAAP. [IAS 18 para 7].
Revenue			
Recognition – general	App Note G of FRS 5 deals with revenue recognition from the supply of goods or services by a seller to its customers. SSAP 9 provides guidance on accounting for long-term contracts, and UITF 40 provides further guidance on service contracts. A seller recognises revenue under an exchange transaction with a customer when, and to the extent that, it obtains the right to consideration in exchange for its performance. [FRS 5 App Note G4].	Section 23 captures all revenue transactions within one of four broad categories: • sale of goods; • rendering of services; • construction contracts; and • use by others of an entity's assets (yielding interest, royalties or dividends). [FRS 102 para 23.1]. Revenue recognition criteria for each of these categories include the probability that the economic benefits associated with the transaction will flow to the entity and that the revenue and costs can be measured reliably. Additional	Same as new UK GAAP; however, IFRS includes a separate standard for construction contracts. [IAS 18 paras 1, 4; IAS 11 para 1].

	Old UK GAAP	New UK GAAP (FRS 102)	IFRS
		recognition criteria apply within each broad category.	
	Where the right to consideration is conditional or contingent on a specified future event or outcome, the occurrence of which is outside the seller's control, no revenue is recognised until this event has occurred. [UITF 40 para 19].	There is no specific guidance on contingent consideration in FRS 102 and, as such, revenue that is contingent on a future event outside the seller's control should be recognised if the general recognition criteria are met.	
Measurement	Revenue is recognised at the fair value of the right to consideration (which is the amount received or receivable in exchange for performance). [FRS 5 App Note G7].	Same as old UK GAAP. Revenue is recognised at the fair value of the consideration received or receivable. [FRS 102 para 23.3].	Same as old and new UK GAAP. [IAS 18 para 9].
Multiple-element arrangements	A contractual arrangement is accounted for as two or more separate transactions only where the commercial substance is that the individual components operate independently of each other – that is, individual components can be identified that represent a separable good or service that the seller can provide to customers, either on a stand-alone basis or as an optional extra. Where a contractual arrangement consists of various components that do not operate independently of each other, the seller accounts for them together, to reflect the seller's performance of its obligations as a whole in obtaining the right to consideration. [FRS 5 App Note G25, G26].	Same as old UK GAAP. The revenue recognition criteria are usually applied separately to each transaction. However, in certain circumstances, it is necessary to separate a transaction into identifiable components in order to reflect the substance of the transaction. Two or more transactions may need to be grouped together if they are linked in such a way that the whole commercial effect cannot be understood without reference to the series of transactions as a whole. [FRS 102 para 23.8].	Same as old and new UK GAAP. [IAS 18 para 13].
Sale of goods	The general revenue recognition criteria above apply. [FRS 5 App Note G].	Similar to old UK GAAP. In addition to the general revenue recognition criteria above, revenue from the sale of goods is recognised when: • the entity has transferred to the buyer the significant risks and rewards of ownership of goods; and • the entity retains neither continuing managerial involvement nor effective control over the goods sold. [FRS 102 para 23.10].	Same as new UK GAAP. [IAS 18 para 14].

	Old UK GAAP	New UK GAAP (FRS 102)	IFRS
Rendering of services	The general revenue recognition criteria apply. A seller may obtain a right to consideration when some, but not all, of its contractual obligations have been fulfilled. Where a seller has partially performed its contractual obligations, it recognises revenue to the extent that it has obtained the right to consideration through its performance. Revenue is recognised according to the substance of the seller's obligations under the contract. [FRS 5 App Note G; UITF 40 para 17].	Similar to old UK GAAP. Service transactions are accounted for under the 'percentage of completion' method where the outcome of a transaction can be reliably estimated (that is, where the stage of completion of the transaction at the end of the period can be measured reliably, and both the costs incurred and the costs to complete the transaction can be measured reliably). Revenue may be recognised on a straight-line basis if the services are performed by an indeterminate number of acts over a specified period of time. Where the outcome of a service transaction cannot be estimated reliably, revenue is only recognised to the extent of recoverable expenses incurred. Recognition of revenue may have to be deferred in instances where a specific act is more significant than any other acts and recognised when the significant act is executed. [FRS 102 paras 23.14-23.16].	Same as new UK GAAP. [IAS 18 paras 20, 25; IAS 11 para 22].
Agreements for the construction of real estate	There is no explicit guidance on agreements for the construction of real estate in UK accounting standards; the scope of SSAP 9 is wider than that of IAS 11. See guidance below on recognising revenue under long-term contracts.	An entity that undertakes the construction of real estate, and that enters into an agreement with one or more buyers, accounts for the agreement as a sale of services using the 'percentage of completion' method if: • the buyer is able to specify the major structural elements of the design of the real estate before construction begins and/or specify major structural changes once construction is in progress; or • the buyer acquires and supplies construction materials, and the entity provides only construction services. [FRS 102 para 23A.14].	Same as new UK GAAP. [IFRIC 15].

	Old UK GAAP	New UK GAAP (FRS 102)	IFRS
Other types of revenue			
Interest on financial assets	Interest is recognised using the effective interest method under FRS 26. [FRS 26 para 9; FRS 29 AG5-AG8]. For entities that have not adopted FRS 26, there is no explicit guidance for calculating interest income, although (by analogy) FRS 4 is often followed.	Interest is recognised using the effective interest method. [FRS 102 para 23.29(a)].	Same as old UK GAAP for FRS 26 reporters and new UK GAAP. [IAS 18 para 30(a); IAS 39 paras 9, AG5-AG8].
Royalties	The terms of the royalty agreement normally indicate when the revenue has been earned. In general, revenue may be recognised on a straight-line basis over the life of the agreement, or on another systematic basis (such as in relation to sales to which the royalty relates). [FRS 5 App Note G4-G10].	Same as old UK GAAP. Royalties are recognised on an accruals basis in accordance with the substance of the relevant agreement. [FRS 102 para 23.29(b)].	Same as old and new UK GAAP. [IAS 18 para 30(b)].
Dividends	Dividends are recognised when the shareholder's right to receive payment is established. [FRS 21 paras 12-13; FRS 25 para 11].	Same as old UK GAAP. [FRS 102 para 23.29(c)].	Same as old and new UK GAAP. [IAS 18 para 30(c)].
Construction and other long-term contracts			
General	Turnover is recognised when, and to the extent that, the entity obtains the right to consideration. This is derived from an assessment of the fair value of the goods or services provided by the reporting date as a proportion of the total fair value of the contract. When the outcome can be assessed with reasonable certainty, the prudently calculated attributable profit is recognised as the difference between the reported turnover and related costs for that contract. [FRS 5 App Note G18, SSAP 9 para 29].	Similar to old UK GAAP. Where the outcome of a contract can be estimated reliably, revenue and costs are recognised by reference to the stage of completion of the contract activity at the end of the reporting period ('percentage of completion' method). Reliable estimation of the outcome requires reliable estimates of the stage of completion, future costs and collectability of billings. [FRS 102 para 23.17].	Similar to new UK GAAP. Additional detailed guidance on fixed price and cost-plus contracts is provided. [IAS 11 paras 22-24; IAS 18 para 21].
'Percentage of completion' method	Where the business carries out long-term contracts, and it is considered that the contracts' outcome can be reliably measured before their conclusion, the attributable profit is calculated on a prudent basis and included in the accounts for the period under review. The profit taken up needs to reflect the proportion of work carried out	Similar to old UK GAAP. The stage of completion of a transaction or contract is determined using the method that measures most reliably the work performed. Where the final outcome cannot be estimated reliably, revenue recognised is limited to the extent of costs	Same as new UK GAAP. [IAS 11 para 32].

	Old UK GAAP	New UK GAAP (FRS 102)	IFRS
	at the accounting date and to take into account any known inequalities of profitability in the various stages of the contract. If it is expected that there will be a loss on a contract as a whole, all of the loss is recognised as soon as it is foreseen. [SSAP 9 para 9].	incurred, if those costs are expected to be recovered (that is, no profit is recognised). When it is probable that total contract costs will exceed total contract revenue, the expected loss is recognised immediately as an expense. [FRS 102 paras 23.21-23.27].	
Combining and segmenting contracts	Long-term contracts should be assessed on a contract-by-contract basis. A contract is accounted for as separate components where the substance is that the individual components operate independently of each other. [SSAP 9 para 28; FRS 5 App Note G25].	Combining and segmenting of contracts is required when certain criteria are met. [FRS 102 paras 23.18-23.20].	Same as new UK GAAP. [IAS 11 paras 8-9].
Other topics			
Barter transactions	UITF 26 applies to 'barter transactions for advertising'. Application of the UITF to barter transactions for services other than advertising is not mandatory; however, its principles of reliable measurement of revenue and costs, and persuasive evidence that the cash value is available, may be relevant to such transactions (although the UITF believes that such evidence will be rare). There is no distinction between similar and dissimilar goods. [UITF 26 paras 4, 10].	Revenue may be recognised on the exchange of dissimilar goods and services. The transaction is measured at the fair value of goods or services received, adjusted by the amount of any cash or cash equivalents transferred. The carrying value of the goods and services given up, adjusted by the amount of any cash or cash equivalents transferred, is used where the fair value of goods or services received or transferred cannot be measured reliably. Exchanges of similar goods and services do not generate revenue. [FRS 102 paras 23.6-23.7].	Similar to new UK GAAP, except that there is no accommodation to use carrying value if fair value cannot be reliably measured. The guidance in SIC-31 applies only to dissimilar advertising services; but, in practice, it is applied (by analogy) to other items. [IAS 18 para 12; SIC-31].
Discounting of revenues	Where the time value of money is material to reported revenue, the amount of revenue recognised is the present value of the cash inflows expected to be received from the customer in settlement. [FRS 5 App Note G9].	Discounting of revenues to present value is required in instances where the inflow of cash or cash equivalents is deferred and the arrangement constitutes, in effect, a financing transaction. In such instances, an imputed interest rate is used for determining the amount of revenue to be recognised, as well as the separate interest income component to be recorded over time. [FRS 102 para 23.5].	Same as new UK GAAP. [IAS 18 para 11].

	Old UK GAAP	New UK GAAP (FRS 102)	IFRS
Government grants			
Definition	Government grants are assistance by government in the form of cash or transfers of assets to an enterprise in return for past or future compliance with certain conditions relating to the operating activities of the enterprise. [SSAP 4 para 22].	Similar to old UK GAAP, except that grants exclude forms of assistance that cannot reasonably be valued or distinguished from normal trading of the entity. [FRS 102 paras 24.1-24.2].	Same as new UK GAAP. [IAS 20 para 3].
Recognition and measurement	Grant income is not recognised unless there is reasonable assurance that the entity will comply with the conditions of the grant and the grant will be received. [SSAP 4 para 24].	New UK GAAP also prohibits recognition of grant income unless there is reasonable assurance that the entity will comply with the conditions of the grant and the grant will be received. [FRS 102 para 24.3A].	Grant income is not recognised until there is a reasonable assurance that the entity will comply with the conditions of the grant and the grant will be received. [IAS 20 para 7].
	Government grants are recognised as income over the periods necessary to match them with the related costs that they are intended to compensate, on a systematic basis (accruals model). Government grants received as compensation for expenses or losses already incurred (or for immediate financial support) are recognised as income in the period in which the grant becomes receivable. [SSAP 4 para 23].	When these criteria are met, entities have a choice between the performance and the accruals model for recognition. [FRS 102 para 24.4]. The accruals model is the same as old UK GAAP. [FRS 102 paras 24.5C-24.5G]. The performance model requires an entity to recognise government grants according to the nature of the grant. There is no distinction between income and capital grants. Recognition is as follows: • A grant that does not impose specified future performance conditions on the recipient is recognised in income when the grant proceeds are receivable. • A grant that imposes specified future performance conditions on the recipient is recognised in income only when the performance conditions are met. • Grants received before the income recognition criteria are satisfied are recognised as a liability and released to income when all attached conditions have been complied with. [FRS 102 para 24.5B].	IFRS also uses an accruals model. [IAS 20 paras 12, 20].

	Old UK GAAP	**New UK GAAP (FRS 102)**	**IFRS**
	Government grants made as a contribution towards expenditure on fixed assets may either be: • treated as deferred income and credited to the profit and loss account over the expected useful economic life of the related asset; or • deducted against the cost of the related asset, with a consequent reduction in the annual deprecation charge. Those applying UK company law are prohibited from applying the second option. [SSAP 4 para 15].	Grants are never deducted against related assets. [FRS 102 para 24.5G].	There are two options: deferred income; or deduction against the related asset. [IAS 20 para 24]. *FRS 101 RDF (IFRS): FRS 101 amends IAS 20 to comply with company law. Grants cannot be deducted against the related assets. [FRS 101 para AG1(m)].*
	Where a government grant takes the form of a transfer of non-monetary assets, the amount of the grant is the fair value of the assets transferred. [SSAP 4 para 16].	Grants are measured at the fair value of the asset received or receivable. [FRS 102 para 24.5].	Non-monetary government grants may be recognised either at fair value or at a nominal amount. [IAS 20 para 23].
Repayment of grants	A government grant that becomes repayable is accounted for as a revision to an accounting estimate (that is, in the current period). Repayment of a grant related to income is applied against any unamortised deferred credit set up in respect of the grant, and then any excess is recognised immediately as an expense. [SSAP 4 para 27].	Where a grant becomes repayable, it is recognised as a liability where the repayment meets the definition of a liability. [FRS 102 para 24.5A].	Same as old and new UK GAAP. [IAS 20 para 32].

Areas covered in IFRS, but not in old UK GAAP or FRS 102, include:

- Extended warranties.
- Transfer of assets from customers (IFRIC 18).

Expenses

	Old UK GAAP	New UK GAAP (FRS 102)	IFRS
Expense recognition – general	Financial statements draw a distinction between changes in ownership interest arising from transactions with owners in their capacity as owners, and other changes. These latter changes are gains and losses. Expenses (losses) are recognised in the income statement (or, as required, in the statement of total recognised gains and losses) where a decrease in ownership interest has occurred. [SoP 4 para 39; FRS 3 para 27].	The recognition of expenses results directly from the recognition and measurement of assets and liabilities. Expenses are recognised in the statement of comprehensive income (or in the income statement, if separately presented) where a decrease in future economic benefits (related to a decrease in an asset or an increase of a liability) has arisen that can be measured reliably. [FRS 102 para 2.42].	Same as new UK GAAP. [IFRS Framework para 4.49].
Borrowing costs	Capitalisation of finance costs is a policy choice. An entity that adopts a policy of capitalising finance costs applies this consistently to all tangible fixed assets where finance costs fall to be capitalised. Only finance costs that are directly attributable to the construction of a tangible fixed asset, or the financing of progress payments in respect of the construction of a tangible fixed asset by others for the entity, are capitalised. [FRS 15 paras 19–21].	Same as old UK GAAP. An entity can adopt a policy of capitalising borrowing costs that are directly attributable to the acquisition, construction or production of a qualifying asset. [FRS 102 para 25.2].	Borrowing costs that are directly attributable to the acquisition, construction or production of a qualifying asset as part of the cost of that asset are capitalised. All other borrowing costs are expensed. [IAS 23 paras 5, 8].

Employee benefits

	Old UK GAAP	New UK GAAP (FRS 102)	IFRS
Employee benefits	FRS 17's scope is limited to retirement benefits only. FRS 17 covers all retirement benefits that an employer is committed to providing, whether the commitment is statutory, contractual or implicit in the employer's actions. [FRS 17 para 4].	Wider in scope than old UK GAAP. Employee benefits are all forms of consideration given by an entity in exchange for services rendered by its employees (except for share-based payments, which are covered by section 26). These benefits include: • short-term employee benefits (such as wages, salaries, profit-sharing and bonuses); • termination benefits (such as severance and redundancy pay);	Same as new UK GAAP. [IAS 19 paras 5, 8].

	Old UK GAAP	New UK GAAP (FRS 102)	IFRS
		• post-employment benefits (such as retirement benefit plans); and • other long-term employee benefits (such as long-term service leave and jubilee benefits). [FRS 102 paras 28.1, 28.2].	
Short-term employee benefits	There is no specific UK accounting standard dealing with benefits such as wages, salaries, bonuses, holidays, maternity leave, benefits in kinds and other short-term benefits. As a result, differing accounting treatments have developed. The principles of FRS 12, 'Provisions, contingent liabilities and contingent assets', have been relevant to the accounting for short-term employee benefits.	Where an employee has rendered services, an expense is recognised for the cost of the undiscounted amount of the short-term employee benefits expected to be paid. [FRS 102 paras 28.3-28.6]. Profit-sharing and bonus payments are recognised where there is a present legal or constructive obligation as a result of past events and a reliable estimate can be made. [FRS 102 para 28.8].	Same as new UK GAAP. [IAS 19 paras 9– 25].
Post-employment benefits – retirement benefits (pensions)			
General	Retirement benefits are provided to employees either through defined contribution schemes or defined benefit schemes. [FRS 17 paras 2, 7, 13].	Same as old UK GAAP. [FRS 102 paras 28.9-28.10].	Same as new UK GAAP. [IAS 19 paras 26-31].
Distinction between defined contribution plans and defined benefit plans	A defined contribution scheme is a pension or other retirement benefit scheme into which an employer pays regular contributions that are fixed as an amount or as a percentage of pay, and under which the employer will have no legal or constructive obligation to pay further contributions if the scheme does not have sufficient assets to pay all employee benefits relating to employee service in the current and prior periods. A defined benefit scheme is a pension or other retirement benefit scheme other than a defined contribution scheme. [FRS 17 para 2].	Same as old UK GAAP. Whether an arrangement is a defined contribution scheme or a defined benefit scheme depends on the substance of the transaction rather than the form of the agreement. [FRS 102 para 28.10].	Same as new UK GAAP. [IAS 19 paras 8, 27-28].
Multi-employer plans	Multi-employer schemes are classified on the basis of the terms of the scheme. In the case of a multi-employer defined benefit scheme, the entity should account for the scheme as defined benefit, unless:	Same as old UK GAAP. [FRS 102 para 28.11].	Same as new UK GAAP. [IAS 19 paras 32-39].

	Old UK GAAP	New UK GAAP (FRS 102)	IFRS
	• contributions relate to only the current period; or • it cannot identify its share of scheme assets and liabilities on a consistent and reasonable basis. If either of these situations applies, the scheme is accounted for as a defined contribution scheme. [FRS 17 paras 8-9].		
	There is currently diversity in practice when accounting for multi-employer schemes with an agreement to fund a deficit relating to past service.	A liability should be recognised where there is an agreement to fund a deficit relating to past service in a multi-employer plan, even though the scheme is otherwise accounted for as a defined contribution scheme. [FRS 102 para 28.11A].	Same as new UK GAAP. [IAS 19 paras 32-39].
Group plans	Group plans are not distinguished from multi-employer plans; therefore, see section on multi-employer plans above for treatment in relation to group schemes. The scheme is considered defined benefit on consolidation. However, this can mean that each entity individually accounts for the scheme as defined contribution. [FRS 17 paras 8–9].	The scheme is considered defined benefit on consolidation, and at least one entity will apply defined benefit scheme accounting, depending on the group policy for charging pension costs around the group. [FRS 102 para 28.38].	Same as new UK GAAP. [IAS 19 paras 40-42].
Insured benefit	Insurance policies that exactly match the amount and timing of some or all of the benefits payable under the scheme are measured at the same amount as the related obligations. For other insurance policies, there are a number of possible valuation methods. The method chosen should give the best approximation to fair value, given the circumstances of the scheme. [FRS 17 para 18].	A post-employment benefit scheme, whose benefits are settled by an insurance contract, is treated as a defined contribution scheme only where the entity has no legal or constructive obligation either: • to pay the employee benefits directly to the employee when they become due; or • to pay further amounts if the insurer does not pay all future employee benefits relating to employee service in the current and prior periods. A constructive obligation could arise indirectly under the plan, through the mechanism for setting future premiums or through a related-party relationship with the insurer. [FRS 102 para 28.12].	Same as new UK GAAP. [IAS 19 paras 46-49].

	Old UK GAAP	New UK GAAP (FRS 102)	IFRS
Defined contribution plans	The cost of a defined contribution scheme is equal to the contributions payable to the scheme for the accounting period. The cost is recognised within operating profit in the profit and loss account. [FRS 17 para 7].	Same as old UK GAAP. Cost is expensed unless recognised as part of the cost of an asset. If contributions paid exceed contributions due, the excess is recognised as an asset to the extent that it will lead to a reduction in future payments or a cash refund. [FRS 102 para 28.13]. Contributions to a defined contribution plan which are not expected to be settled wholly within 12 months after the end of the period should be measured at the present value of the contributions payable. [FRS 102 para 28.13A].	Same as new UK GAAP. [IAS 19 paras 51-52].
Defined benefit plans	The net defined benefit liability/(asset) is the net total of: ● the present value of the defined benefit obligation at the end of the reporting period;	The net defined benefit liability/(asset) is the net total of: ● the present value of the defined benefit obligation at the end of the reporting period;	The net defined benefit liability/(asset) is the net total of: ● the present value of the defined benefit obligation at the end of the reporting period.
	● minus the fair value at the reporting date of plan assets (if any) out of which the obligations are to be settled directly;	● minus the fair value at the reporting date of plan assets (if any) out of which the obligations are to be settled directly.	● minus the fair value at the reporting date of plan assets (if any) out of which the obligations are to be settled directly.
	● minus any unrecognised past-service costs.	● Not applicable.	● Not applicable.
	[FRS 17 paras 37, 60].	[FRS 102 para 28.15].	[IAS 19 para 120-126].
Asset recoverability	An entity recognises a plan surplus as a defined benefit asset only to the extent that it is recoverable through reduced future contributions or refunds from the plan. [FRS 17 para 37]. The amounts to be recovered from refunds should only reflect refunds that have been agreed at the balance sheet date. [FRS 17 para 42].	Similar to old UK GAAP, except it is not necessary to have trustee agreement at the balance sheet date. [FRS 102 para 28.22].	Same as new UK GAAP, in that there is no restriction regarding the timing of the refunds. [IAS 19 paras 63-65]. Detailed guidance on determining the economic benefit available from future contributions is provided in IFRIC 14.
Minimum funding requirements	Not specifically addressed in FRS 17.	An entity does not recognise any additional minimum funding liabilities arising from a funding agreement with its defined benefit plan, unless it is a multi-employer scheme which it is accounting for as defined contribution. [FRS 102 paras 28.11A, 28.15A].	A minimum funding requirement may give rise to additional liabilities. [IFRIC 14 paras 23, 24].

	Old UK GAAP	New UK GAAP (FRS 102)	IFRS
Components of the cost of a defined benefit plan	The changes in the net defined benefit asset or liability (other than those arising from contributions to the scheme) are analysed into the following components: Periodic costs: • current service cost; • interest cost; • expected return of asset; and • actuarial gains and losses. Non-periodic costs: • past-service cost; and • gains and losses on curtailments and settlements. [FRS 17 para 50].	Similar to old UK GAAP. However, instead of applying the discount rate to the liability and an expected return to the asset, the net interest cost is derived by multiplying the net defined benefit obligation (surplus) by the discount rate, both determined at the start of the period and taking account of any changes in the net defined benefit obligation (surplus) during the period. [FRS 102 para 28.24].	Under IAS 19, net interest is determined on the same basis as that in FRS 102. [IAS 19 paras 123-126].
Actuarial valuation method	Defined benefit scheme liabilities are measured on an actuarial basis using the projected unit credit method. This method sees each period of service as giving rise to an additional unit of benefit entitlement and measures each unit separately to build up the final obligation. [FRS 17 para 20].	Same as old UK GAAP. [FRS 102 paras 28.18-28.20].	Same as new UK GAAP. [IAS 19 paras 56-60].
	Full actuarial valuations by a professionally qualified actuary are required at least every three years. [FRS 17 para 35].	Involvement of an independent actuary is not required when performing a comprehensive actuarial valuation. Valuations are not required annually. [FRS 102 paras 28.18-28.20].	Same as new UK GAAP. Although involvement of a qualified actuary is encouraged, it is not required. Valuations are not required annually. [IAS 19 para 59].
Actuarial gains and losses	Actuarial gains and losses arising from any new valuation, and from updating the latest actuarial valuation to reflect conditions at the balance sheet date, are recognised in full in the statement of total recognised gains and losses for the period. [FRS 17 para 57].	Actuarial gains and losses are recognised in other comprehensive income (without recycling) as 'remeasurements' of the net defined benefit obligation. [FRS 102 paras 28.25-28.26].	IAS 19 is the same as new UK GAAP: actuarial gains and losses ('remeasurements') are recognised immediately in other comprehensive income.
Discount rate	The obligation is discounted at a rate that reflects the time value of money and the characteristics of the liability. Such a rate is assumed to be the	Similar to old UK GAAP. The defined benefit obligation is recorded at present value, using a discount rate derived from high-quality corporate	Same as new UK GAAP. [IAS 19 para 83].

	Old UK GAAP	New UK GAAP (FRS 102)	IFRS
	current rate of return on a high-quality corporate bond of equivalent currency and term to the scheme liabilities. [FRS 17 para 32].	bonds with a maturity consistent with the expected maturity of the obligations. In countries where no deep market in high-quality bonds exists, the yield rate on government bonds is used. [FRS 102 para 28.17].	
Fair value of plan assets	Plan assets are measured at fair value. For quoted securities, the current bid price is taken as the fair value. For unquoted securities, an estimate of fair value is used. [FRS 17 para 14, 16].	Same as old UK GAAP. [FRS 102 paras 28.15(b), 11.27-11.32]. In addition, if the asset is an insurance policy that exactly matches the amount and timing of some or all of the defined benefits payable under the plan, the fair value of the asset is deemed to be the present value of the related obligation. [FRS 102 para 28.15(b)].	Same as new UK GAAP. [IAS 19 para 113].
Reimbursements	Not addressed.	If an entity is virtually certain that another party will reimburse some or all of a defined benefit obligation, it recognises the reimbursement right as a separate asset. The asset is treated in the same way as plan assets. [FRS 102 para 28.28].	Same as new UK GAAP. [IAS 19 paras 116-119].
Expected return on plan assets	The expected return on assets is based on long-term expectations at the beginning of the period and is expected to be reasonably stable. In addition, the expected return on assets reflects changes in the assets in the scheme during the period as a result of contributions paid into and benefits paid out of the scheme. The expected rate of return should be set by management having taken advice from an actuary. [FRS 17 para 54].	Instead of separately determining an expected return on assets and applying the discount rate to the liability, a net interest cost is derived by multiplying the net defined benefit obligation by the discount rate, both at the start of the period and taking account of any changes in the net defined benefit obligation during the period as a result of contributions and benefit payments. [FRS 102 para 28.24].	IAS 19 is the same as new UK GAAP. [IAS 19 para 120].
Past-service costs/benefits	Past-service costs are recognised in the profit and loss account on a straight-line basis over the period in which the increases in benefit vest. To the extent that the benefits vest immediately, the past-service costs are recognised immediately. Any unrecognised past-service costs are deducted from the scheme liabilities and the balance sheet asset or liability, adjusted accordingly. [FRS 17 para 60].	Past-service costs are recognised in full in profit or loss in the period in which they occur. [FRS 102 paras 28.16, 28.21, 28.21A].	IAS 19 is the same as new UK GAAP. [IAS 19 para 103].

	Old UK GAAP	New UK GAAP (FRS 102)	IFRS
Curtailments and settlements	Losses arising on a settlement or curtailment, that are not allowed for in the actuarial assumptions, are measured at the date on which the employer becomes demonstrably committed to the transaction; they are recognised in the profit and loss account covering that date (this may be before the settlement/curtailment date). [FRS 17 para 64].	Losses on the curtailment or settlement of a defined benefit plan are recognised in profit or loss when the curtailment or settlement occurs. [FRS 102 paras 28.21, 28.21A].	Similar to new UK GAAP; however, IFRS includes more detailed guidance in clarifying the terms 'curtailment' and 'settlement'. [IAS 19 paras 102-112].
	Gains arising on a settlement or curtailment, that are not allowed for in the actuarial assumptions, are measured at the date on which all parties whose consent is required are irrevocably committed to the transaction, and they are recognised in the profit and loss account covering that date (this may not be until the curtailment/ settlement date). [FRS 17 para 64].	Similar to losses, gains are also recognised when the curtailment or settlement occurs. For gains, this may be earlier than under old UK GAAP, as there is no 'irrevocably committed' requirement. [FRS 102 para 28.21].	Same as new UK GAAP. [IAS 19 paras 102-112]. In addition, under IAS 19, gains or losses related to plan amendments, curtailments and termination benefits that occur with a restructuring are required to be recognised when the related restructuring costs are recognised, if that is earlier than the normal IAS 19 recognition date. [IAS 19 para 103].
Other long-term employee benefits			
Other long-term employee benefits	Old UK GAAP does not specifically address other long-term employee benefits (other than retirement benefits). As a result, differing accounting treatments have developed. In practice, FRS 12, 'Provisions, contingent assets and contingent liabilities', has been used to deal with employee benefits other than retirement benefits.	Other long-term benefits include long-service and sabbatical leave, jubilee and other long-service benefits, long-term disability benefits and compensation, and bonus payments not expected to be settled wholly before 12 months after the end of the period in which they are earned. The amount recognised as a liability for other long-term benefits is the net of: ● the present value of the benefit obligation at the reporting date; ● less the fair value at the reporting date of plan assets (if any) out of which the obligations are to be settled directly. The change in the present value of the obligation is normally recorded in the income statement. Nothing is taken via other comprehensive income. [FRS 102 paras 28.29-28.30].	Same as new UK GAAP. [IAS 19 paras 153-158].
Termination benefits			
Recognition	Old UK GAAP does not specifically address employee benefits other than retirement benefits.	Termination benefits are recorded when management is demonstrably committed to the reduction in workforce. Management is	Similar to new UK GAAP. However, IFRS includes further guidance on the minimum

	Old UK GAAP	New UK GAAP (FRS 102)	IFRS
	In practice, applying the principles of FRS 12, termination benefits are recognised where there is a present legal or constructive obligation as a result of past events and a reliable estimate can be made. Because there is no future economic benefit, the expense is recognised immediately.	demonstrably committed to a termination only when it is committed to terminate employment prior to normal retirement date or to provide benefits under voluntary redundancy offers made. In addition, management must have a detailed formal plan for the termination that is without realistic possibility of withdrawal. Termination benefits do not provide an entity with future economic benefits and are recognised as an expense immediately. [FRS 102 paras 28.31-28.35].	requirement of a detailed plan. [IAS 19 paras 159-164]. IAS 19 explicitly requires that any benefit that must be earned by working for a future period is not a termination benefit. A termination benefit is given only in exchange for the termination of employment. [IAS 19 paras 159-164].
Measurement	Old UK GAAP does not specifically address other long-term employee benefits (other than retirement benefits). As a result, differing accounting treatments have developed. In practice, the principles of FRS 12 are applied such that the entity provides the best estimate of the expenditure required to settle the obligation. Where termination benefits are due more than 12 months after the balance sheet date, an entity discounts them.	Termination benefits are measured at the best estimate of the expenditure that would be required to settle the obligation at the reporting date. In the case of an offer made to encourage voluntary redundancy, the measurement of termination benefits is based on the number of employees expected to accept the offer. Where termination benefits are due more than 12 months after the end of the reporting period, they are measured at their discounted present value. [FRS 102 paras 28.36-28.37].	Similar to new UK GAAP. [IAS 19 para 169].

Share-based payments

	Old UK GAAP	New UK GAAP (FRS 102)	IFRS
Scope	Share-based payment transactions include equity-settled and cash-settled share-based payments. [FRS 20 paras 2-6]. FRS 20 is identical to IFRS 2.	Same as old UK GAAP. [FRS 102 para 26.1].	Same as old UK GAAP and new UK GAAP. [IFRS 2 paras 2-6].
Recognition	An entity recognises the goods or services received in a share-based payment transaction when it obtains the goods or as services are received. [FRS 20 para 7].	Same as old UK GAAP. [FRS 102 para 26.3].	Same as old UK GAAP and new UK GAAP. [IFRS 2 para 7].

	Old UK GAAP	New UK GAAP (FRS 102)	IFRS
Measurement – equity-settled share-based transactions	Transactions are measured at fair value of the goods or services received. If the entity cannot estimate reliably these fair values (which is always deemed to be the case for transactions with employees), the transactions are measured at the fair value of the equity instruments granted, ignoring any service or non-market vesting conditions or reload features.	Same as old UK GAAP. [FRS 102 para 26.7].	Same as old UK GAAP and new UK GAAP. [IFRS 2 para 10].
	Market conditions are taken into account when estimating the fair value of the equity instruments granted. For grants of equity instruments with market conditions, the entity recognises the goods or services received from a counterparty that satisfies all other vesting conditions, irrespective of whether that market condition is satisfied.	Same as old UK GAAP. [FRS 102 para 26.9].	Same as old UK GAAP and new UK GAAP. [IFRS 2 para 21].
	Similarly, an entity takes into account all non-vesting conditions when estimating the fair value of the equity instruments granted. [FRS 20 paras 10, 21, 21A].	Same as old UK GAAP. [FRS 102 para 26.9].	Same as old UK GAAP and new UK GAAP. [IFRS 2 para 21A].
	The fair value of equity instruments granted is measured, based on market prices (if available), taking into account the terms and conditions on which those equity instruments were granted (as noted above). If market prices are not available, the fair value is determined using a valuation technique to estimate the price of those equity instruments. The valuation technique should be consistent with generally accepted valuation methodologies for pricing financial instruments, and should incorporate all factors and assumptions that knowledgeable, willing market participants would consider in setting the price. [FRS 20 paras 16-18, App B].	FRS 102 specifies a three-tier hierarchy that is applied when measuring the fair value of the equity instruments: 1. use of observable market prices; 2. use of specific observable market data, such as a recent transaction in the equity instruments or a recent independent fair valuation of the entity; and 3. use of a generally accepted valuation technique that uses market data to the greatest extent practicable. For shares, the entity's directors should use their judgement to apply a generally accepted valuation methodology for valuing equity instruments that is appropriate to the circumstances of the entity. For share options, any option pricing model used should include the inputs specified by the standard. [FRS 102 paras 26.10-26.11].	Same as old UK GAAP. [IFRS 2 paras 16-18, App B].

	Old UK GAAP	New UK GAAP (FRS 102)	IFRS
Vesting conditions	Vesting conditions, other than market conditions, are not taken into account when estimating the fair value of the equity instruments granted. Instead, vesting conditions are taken into account when estimating the number of equity instruments expected to vest. Subsequently, the estimate is revised so that, ultimately, it equals the number of equity instruments that eventually vest. [FRS 20 para 19].	Same as old UK GAAP. [FRS 102 para 26.9].	Same as old UK GAAP and new UK GAAP. [IFRS 2 para 19].
Measurement – cash-settled share-based transaction	Cash-settled share-based payment transactions are measured at the fair value of the liability. Until the liability is settled, the fair value of the liability is remeasured at each reporting date and at the date of final settlement, with any changes in fair value recognised in profit or loss. [FRS 20 para 30].	Same as old UK GAAP. [FRS 102 para 26.14].	Same as old UK GAAP and new UK GAAP. [IFRS 2 para 30].
Share-based payment transactions with cash alternatives	For share-based payment transactions where the entity has a choice of settlement in cash (or other assets) or by issuing equity instruments, the entity accounts for the transaction as cash-settled if: • the choice of settlement in equity instruments has no commercial substance; or • the entity has a past practice or a stated policy of settling in cash, or generally settles in cash whenever the counterparty asks for cash settlement. Otherwise, it accounts for the transaction as equity-settled. [FRS 20 paras 34, 41-43].	Same as old UK GAAP where the entity has a choice of settlement. [FRS 102 para 26.15A].	Same as old UK GAAP. [IFRS 2 paras 34, 41-43].
	Where the counterparty has a choice of settlement in cash (or other assets) or by issuing equity instruments, the entity accounts for a compound financial instrument, which includes a debt component and an equity component. [FRS 20 paras 34, 35-40].	When the counterparty has a choice of settlement in cash (or other assets) or by the transfer of equity instruments, the entity accounts for the transaction as wholly cash-settled, unless the choice of settlement in cash (or other assets) has no commercial substance (in which case it is accounted for as wholly equity-settled). [FRS 102 para 26.15A].	Same as old UK GAAP. [IFRS 2 paras 34, 35-40].

	Old UK GAAP	New UK GAAP (FRS 102)	IFRS
Group share-based payment awards	Share-based payment awards that are granted by an entity in the group, other than by the entity receiving the goods or services, are recognised in both sets of individual and consolidated financial statements. [FRS 20 para 43A]. The entity receiving the goods or services will recognise an expense in respect of the benefit received. The award is accounted for as an equity-settled share-based payment transaction where: • the awards granted are the entity's own equity instruments; or • the entity has no obligation to settle the share-based payment transaction. Otherwise, the award is accounted for as a cash-settled share-based payment transaction. [FRS 20 para 43B]. For the entity that is settling the award where another entity in the group receives the goods or services, the transaction is accounted for as an equity-settled share-based payment transaction only where it is settled in the entity's own equity instruments. Otherwise, it is accounted for as a cash-settled share-based payment transaction. [FRS 20 para 43C].	The employing entity is permitted, as an alternative to the above accounting, to recognise and measure the share-based payment expense on the basis of a reasonable allocation of the expense for the group. [FRS 102 para 26.16].	Same as old UK GAAP. [IFRS 2 paras 43A-43D].

Income taxes

	Old UK GAAP	New UK GAAP (FRS 102)	IFRS
Scope	The standard applies to taxes calculated on the basis of taxable profits, including withholding taxes paid on behalf of the reporting entity. [FRS 19 para 4].	Similar to old UK GAAP. Income tax includes all taxes that are based on taxable profit, and taxes (such as withholding taxes) that are payable by a subsidiary, associate or joint venture on distributions to the reporting entity. [FRS 102 para 29.1]. FRS 102 also includes guidance on accounting for VAT and other similar sales taxes. [FRS 102 para 29.2A].	Same as new UK GAAP. [IAS 12 para 2].

	Old UK GAAP	**New UK GAAP (FRS 102)**	**IFRS**
Current taxes			
Definition	Current tax is the amount of tax estimated to be payable or recoverable in respect of the taxable profit or loss for the period, along with adjustments to estimates in respect of previous periods. [FRS 16 para 2].	Similar to old UK GAAP. The amount of income tax payable (refundable) in respect of the taxable profit (tax loss) for the current period or past periods. [FRS 102 para 29.2].	Similar to new UK GAAP, although past periods are not referred to. [IAS 12 para 5].
Recognition	Current tax is recognised in the profit and loss account for the period, except to the extent that it is attributable to a gain or loss that is or has been recognised directly in the statement of total recognised gains and losses. [FRS 16 para 5].	Unpaid current tax for current and prior periods is recognised as a liability. If the amount already paid exceeds the amount due for those periods, the excess is recognised as an asset. The benefit relating to a tax loss that can be carried back to recover current tax of a previous period is recognised as an asset. [FRS 102 paras 29.3-29.4].	Same as new UK GAAP. [IAS 12 paras 12-13].
Measurement	Current tax is measured at the amounts expected to be paid (or recovered) using the tax rates and laws that have been enacted or substantively enacted by the balance sheet date. [FRS 16 para 14].	Similar to old UK GAAP. Current taxes are not discounted. [FRS 102 paras 29.5, 29.17].	Similar to new UK GAAP, except that IAS 12 is silent on the discounting of current tax. Whether discounting is applied or not is an accounting policy choice. [IAS 12 para 46].
Deferred taxes			
Approach	Follows a 'timing difference' approach.	Follows a 'timing differences plus' approach.	Follows a 'temporary difference' approach.
Definition	Deferred tax is the estimated future tax consequences of transactions and events recognised in the financial statements of the current and previous periods. [FRS 19 para 2].	Same as old UK GAAP. [FRS 102 para 29.2].	Deferred tax is the amount of income taxes payable (potentially recoverable) in the future in respect of taxable (deductible) temporary differences (and the carry-forward of unused tax losses and tax credits). [IAS 12 para 5].
Temporary difference	There is no concept of a 'temporary difference' in old UK GAAP.	There is no concept of a 'temporary difference' in FRS 102, although a similar approach is used for deferred tax relating to business combinations (see below).	Fundamentally different from old UK GAAP and different from new UK GAAP. A temporary difference is the difference between the carrying amount of an asset or liability and its tax base. [IAS 12 para 5]. The tax base of an asset or liability is determined based on the expected manner of recovery (for example, either sale or use, or a combination of both) or settlement; except for investment property, where there is a rebuttable presumption

	Old UK GAAP	New UK GAAP (FRS 102)	IFRS
			that it will be recovered through sale. [IAS 12 paras 51A, 51C].
Timing difference	Timing differences are differences between an entity's taxable profits and its results that arise from the inclusion of gains and losses in tax assessments in periods different from those in which they are recognised in financial statements. [FRS 19 para 2].	Same as old UK GAAP. [FRS 102 para 29.6]	There is no separate concept of a 'timing difference' in IFRS; these are covered under temporary differences.
Recognition of deferred tax	Deferred tax is recognised on the basis of timing differences (subject to certain exceptions). [FRS 19 para 7].	Can differ from old UK GAAP. Deferred tax is recognised in respect of all timing differences at the balance sheet date, except as otherwise specified. [FRS 102 para 29.6].	Deferred tax is recognised on the basis of temporary differences (subject to certain exceptions, including on the initial recognition of an asset or liability in a transaction that is not a business combination and, at the time of the transaction, affects neither accounting nor tax profit). [IAS 12 para 15].
Permanent differences	Permanent differences are differences between an entity's taxable profits and its results as stated in the financial statements, that arise because certain types of income and expenditure are non-taxable or disallowable, or because certain tax charges or allowances have no corresponding amount in the financial statements. Deferred tax is not recognised on permanent differences. [FRS 19 para 7(b)].	Same as old UK GAAP, except for deferred tax relating to business combinations. [FRS 102 para 29.10].	There is no separate concept of a 'permanent difference' in IFRS. Temporary differences include all timing differences and many permanent differences, and therefore deferred tax might arise, unless covered by the initial recognition exception.
Deferred tax assets	A deferred tax asset is recognised on timing differences and tax losses to the extent that it is regarded as more likely than not that the deferred tax asset will be recovered. [FRS 19 para 23].	Similar to old UK GAAP. The criteria for recognition are the same, but there is less guidance on determining the availability of future profits. [FRS 102 para 29.7].	Similar to old and new UK GAAP. The carrying amount of the deferred tax asset is reviewed at each reporting date and is reduced when it is no longer probable that sufficient taxable profit will be available to allow recovery of the deferred tax asset. This reduction is reversed when it subsequently becomes probable that sufficient taxable profit will be available. [IAS 12 para 56].
Assets carried at fair value	Deferred tax is recognised on timing differences arising when an asset is continuously revalued to fair value, with changes in fair value being recognised in the profit and loss account. [FRS 19 paras 12-13]. Deferred tax is not recognised on timing differences arising when other non-monetary	Differs from old UK GAAP: deferred tax is recognised on timing differences arising on the revaluation of an asset, including non-monetary asset revaluations through other comprehensive income.	Similar to new UK GAAP, the difference between the carrying amount of an asset carried at fair value and its tax base is a temporary difference, although the initial recognition exception may apply. [IAS 12 para 20].

	Old UK GAAP	New UK GAAP (FRS 102)	IFRS
	assets are revalued, unless the reporting entity has, by the balance sheet date: • entered into a binding agreement to sell the revalued assets; and • recognised the gains and losses expected to arise on sale. [FRS 19 para 14].		
Unremitted earnings of subsidiaries, associates and joint ventures	Deferred tax is recognised only to the extent that: • dividends from a subsidiary, associate or joint venture have been accrued as receivable at the balance sheet; or • a binding agreement to distribute the past earnings in future has been made. [FRS 19 para 21].	Differs from old UK GAAP: deferred tax is recognised when income or expenses from a subsidiary, associate, branch or joint venture have been recognised in the financial statements, and will be assessed to or allowed for tax in a future period, except where: • the reporting entity is able to control the reversal of the timing difference; and • it is probable that the timing difference will not reverse in the foreseeable future. [FRS 102 para 29.9].	Deferred tax is recognised on the unremitted earnings of subsidiaries, branches, associates and joint ventures, except where: • the parent/investor is able to control the timing of the remittance of the earnings; and • it is probable that remittance will not take place in the foreseeable future. [IAS 12 para 39].
Business combinations	Generally, no deferred tax arises on business combinations. Deferred tax can arise on adjustments to record an acquired entity's assets and liabilities at their fair values; these are treated in the same way as they would be if they were timing differences arising in the acquiring entity's own financial statements (for example, deferred tax on upward revaluations of property is only recognised if there is a binding sale agreement). [FRS 7 para 74].	Differs from old UK GAAP: where the amount attributed for tax purposes to assets (other than goodwill) and liabilities that are acquired in a business combination differs from their fair value, deferred tax is recognised to reflect the future tax consequences with a corresponding adjustment to goodwill. [FRS 102 para 29.11].	Similar to new UK GAAP. Deferred tax is provided on the difference between the fair value and tax base of identifiable assets and liabilities acquired in a business combination. [IAS 12 para 19].
Measurement	Deferred tax is measured using tax rates that have been enacted or substantively enacted at the balance sheet date and that are expected to apply in the periods in which the timing differences are expected to reverse. [FRS 19 para 37].	Same as old UK GAAP. [FRS 102 para 29.12].	Similar to old and new UK GAAP. Deferred tax is measured using tax rates that have been enacted or substantively enacted at the balance sheet date and that are expected to apply in the periods in which an asset is recovered or a liability is settled. [IAS 12 para 47].

	Old UK GAAP	**New UK GAAP (FRS 102)**	**IFRS**
	Not applicable.	Deferred tax on a revalued non-depreciable asset (for instance, land) is measured using the tax rates and allowances that apply on sale of the asset. [FRS 102 para 29.15]. Deferred tax on an investment property held at fair value is measured using the tax rates and allowances that apply on sale of the asset, unless the property is held in a business model where substantially all of the property's economic benefits will be consumed over time. [FRS 102 para 29.16].	Generally, the measurement of deferred tax reflects the tax consequences that would follow from the manner in which the entity expects, at the end of the reporting period, to recover or settle the carrying amount of its assets and liabilities. There are exceptions for revalued non-depreciable assets and investment property, which are similar to new UK GAAP. [IAS 12 para 51].
	Reporting entities are permitted, but not required, to discount deferred tax assets and liabilities to reflect the time value of money. [FRS 19 para 42].	Can differ from old UK GAAP, because deferred tax assets and liabilities are not discounted. [FRS 102 para 29.17].	Deferred tax assets and liabilities are not discounted. [IAS 12 para 53].
Other topics			
Withholding tax on dividend	Outgoing dividends are recognised at an amount that includes any withholding taxes. [FRS 16 para 8].	Tax relating to dividends that is paid or payable to taxation authorities on behalf of the shareholders (for example, withholding tax) is charged to equity as part of the dividends. [FRS 102 para 29.18].	Same as new UK GAAP. [IAS 12 para 65A].
Uncertain tax position	There is no specific guidance on uncertain tax positions under FRS 16 or FRS 19. In practice, entities have to make an accounting policy choice as to whether an uncertain tax position is measured as either a single best estimate or a probability-weighted average of the possible outcomes, if the likelihood is greater than 50%.	Same as old UK GAAP.	Same as old UK GAAP and new UK GAAP.
Offsetting	Deferred tax assets and liabilities are offset only if they: • relate to taxes levied by the same tax authority; and • arise in the same taxable entity or different taxable entities within a tax group. The same approach applies to current taxes. [FRS 19 paras 56-57].	Similar to old UK GAAP, although there must be an intention, as well as a right, to offset. [FRS 102 paras 29.24-29.24A].	Same as new UK GAAP. [IAS 12 paras 71, 74-75].

	Old UK GAAP	New UK GAAP (FRS 102)	IFRS
Recognition in the performance statements or directly in equity	Current and deferred tax is recognised in the profit and loss account for the period, except to the extent that it is attributable to a gain or loss that is or has been recognised directly in the statement of total recognised gains and losses. In this case, the deferred tax attributable to that gain or loss is also recognised directly in the statement of total recognised gains and losses. Tax is not recognised directly in equity. [FRS 16 paras 5-6; FRS 19 paras 34-35].	Can differ from old UK GAAP. Current and deferred tax is recognised in the same component of total comprehensive income (that is, continuing or discontinued operations, and profit or loss or other comprehensive income) or equity as the transaction or other event that resulted in the tax expense, except for deferred tax arising on the initial recognition of a business combination which is recognised via goodwill. [FRS 102 paras 29.21-29.22].	Same as new UK GAAP. [IAS 12 paras 58, 61A, 68].
Disclosure	A reconciliation is required of the current tax charge or credit on ordinary activities to the current tax charge, or credit that would result from applying the standard rate of tax to the profit on ordinary activities before tax. Either the monetary amounts or the rates (as a percentage of profit on ordinary activities before tax) may be reconciled. [FRS 19 para 64(a)].	FRS 102 disclosures include a reconciliation between the total tax expense or income (current and deferred) and the profit or loss on ordinary activities before taxation, multiplied by the applicable rate of tax. [FRS 102 para 29.27(b)].	Same as new UK GAAP. Either the monetary amounts or the rates (as a percentage of profit on ordinary activities before tax) may be reconciled. [IAS 12 para 81(c)].
		FRS 102 includes a requirement to disclose expected net reversals of deferred tax balances in the next year. [FRS 102 para 29.27(c)].	

Areas covered in IFRS, but not in FRS 102, include:

- Reassessment of unrecognised deferred tax assets.
- Tax planning opportunities.
- Current and deferred tax arising from share-based payment transactions.
- Exchange differences on deferred foreign tax liabilities or assets.

3. Balance sheet and related notes

Intangible assets

	Old UK GAAP	New UK GAAP (FRS 102)	IFRS
Definition	An intangible asset is a non-financial fixed asset that does not have physical substance, but is identifiable and is controlled by the entity through custody or legal rights. [FRS 10 para 2]. An intangible asset is identifiable where it can be disposed of separately from the revenue-earning activity to which it contributes. Separability is a necessary condition for identifiability. [FRS 10 para 2].	An intangible asset is an identifiable non-monetary asset without physical substance. The identifiable criterion is met when an intangible asset is separable (that is, it can be sold, transferred, licensed, rented or exchanged), or where it arises from contractual or legal rights. [FRS 102 para 18.2].	Same as new UK GAAP. [IAS 38 paras 8,11-12].
General principles for recognition	An internally developed intangible asset can be capitalised only if it has a readily ascertainable market value. If its value cannot be measured reliably, an intangible asset purchased as part of the acquisition of a business is subsumed within the amount of the purchase price attributed to goodwill. [FRS 10 paras 13, 14].	Expenditure on intangibles is recognised as an asset when it meets the recognition criteria of an asset. [FRS 102 paras 18.4-18.7].	Same as new UK GAAP. [IAS 38 paras 21-23].
Recognition as an expense	Expenditure on the following items is not recognised as an asset: • start-up costs; • training; • advertising; and • relocation costs. [UITF 24].	Same as old UK GAAP. [FRS 102 para 18.8C].	Same as old UK GAAP and new UK GAAP. [IAS 38 para 69].
	The cost of an internally generated intangible asset is the sum of expenditure incurred from the date when the intangible asset first meets the recognition criteria. Reinstatement of expenditure previously recognised as an expense is prohibited (for example, as in UITF 34, 'Pre-contract costs').	Internally generated intangibles are expensed. The following are listed as examples: • brands; • logos; • customer lists; • publishing titles; and	Same as new UK GAAP. [IAS 38 para 63].

	Old UK GAAP	New UK GAAP (FRS 102)	IFRS
	Website development costs, incurred by companies in developing websites for their own use, are capitalised as a tangible fixed asset, subject to specific criteria being met for the capitalisation of design and content costs. [UITF 29].	• items similar in substance. [FRS 102 para 18.8C]. Past expenses on intangible items are not recognised as an asset. [FRS 102 para 18.17].	
Initial measurement			
Separately acquired intangible assets	Capitalise at cost. There is no explanation of what cost includes. [FRS 10 para 9].	Same as old UK GAAP. Intangible assets are measured initially at cost. Cost includes: • the purchase price; and • any costs directly attributable to preparing the asset for its intended use. [FRS 102 paras 18.9-18.10].	Same as old UK GAAP and new UK GAAP. [IAS 38 paras 24, 27].
Intangible assets acquired as part of a business combination	Judgement is required to determine whether cost (that is, fair value) can be measured sufficiently reliably for the purpose of separate recognition. [FRS 10 para 10]. FRS 10 indicates the techniques that are used to value intangibles where no readily ascertainable market value exists. [FRS 10 para 12]. If its value cannot be measured reliably, an intangible asset purchased as part of the acquisition of a business is subsumed within the amount of the purchase price attributed to goodwill.	The cost of an intangible asset acquired as a part of a business combination is its fair value at the acquisition date. [FRS 102 para 18.11]. Due to the detailed guidance on recognition of intangibles, compared to old UK GAAP, we expect more intangibles to be recognised when applying FRS 102.	Same as new UK GAAP. [IAS 38 para 33].
Research and development costs	Research expenditure is expensed when incurred. [SSAP 13 para 24].	Same as old UK GAAP. [FRS 102 para 18.8E].	Same as old UK GAAP and new UK GAAP. [IAS 38 para 54].
	SSAP 13 allows an option to capitalise development expenditure, provided specific criteria are met: • There is a clearly defined project. • Related expenditure is separately identifiable. • Technical feasibility is reasonably certain.	FRS 102 allows an option to capitalise development expenditure, provided specific criteria are met. The criteria are similar to old UK GAAP, but are more stringent, because there is a requirement to demonstrate future benefits, rather than to have a reasonable expectation of future benefits under SSAP 13. [FRS 102 para 18.8H].	Same criteria as new UK GAAP. If the criteria are met, development expenditure is capitalised. [IAS 38 para 57].

	Old UK GAAP	New UK GAAP (FRS 102)	IFRS
	• It is commercially viable. • Any further costs are reasonably expected to be exceeded by related future revenues. • Adequate resources exist to complete the project. [SSAP 13 para 25].		
Subsequent measurement			
Measurement after initial recognition	The cost or revaluation methods are applied. Where an intangible asset has a readily ascertainable market value, the asset may be revalued to its market value. If one intangible asset is revalued, all other capitalised intangible assets of the same class are revalued. Once an intangible asset has been revalued, further revaluations are performed sufficiently often to ensure that the carrying value does not differ materially from the market value at the balance sheet date. [FRS 10 para 43].	Same as old UK GAAP. Intangible assets may be carried at either cost less any accumulated amortisation and any accumulated impairment losses (cost model) or revaluation model (provided that fair value can be determined by reference to an active market) where intangible assets are carried at a revalued amount, being fair value at the date of revaluation, less any accumulated depreciation and subsequent accumulated impairment losses. [FRS 102 paras 18.18, 18.18A, 18.18B].	Similar to old UK GAAP and new UK GAAP. In addition to the cost model, the revaluation model is an option in which intangible assets are carried at a revalued amount less any accumulated depreciation and subsequent accumulated impairment losses. [IAS 38 paras 72, 75-87].
Useful life	There is a rebuttable presumption that the useful economic life of an intangible asset does not exceed 20 years; however, a longer or indefinite life is permitted. [FRS 10 para 19]. Criteria are provided for rebuttal of the presumption. These are the demonstration of durability and the ability to continue to measure for impairment.	The useful life of an intangible asset is considered to be finite. In exceptional cases, if a reliable estimate is not possible, the life should not exceed five years (increased to 10 years under the July 2015 amendments to FRS 102). [FRS 102 para 18.20]. It is expected that entities transitioning from old UK GAAP to FRS 102 will maintain their existing life for definite-lived intangible assets and goodwill. The useful life of an intangible asset that arises from contractual or other legal rights does not exceed the period of the contractual or other legal rights. However, it may be shorter, depending on the period over which the asset is expected to be used. [FRS 102 para 18.19].	The useful life of an intangible asset is either finite or indefinite. The useful life is regarded as indefinite when, based on analysis of all of the relevant factors, there is no foreseeable limit to the period over which the asset is expected to generate net cash inflows. Similar to new UK GAAP, with regard to the useful life of an intangible asset that arises from contractual or other legal rights, except that renewal periods may be taken into account if certain criteria are met.
Intangible assets with finite useful life	Where goodwill and intangible assets are regarded as having limited useful economic lives, they are amortised on a systematic basis over those lives. [FRS 10 para 15].	Same as old UK GAAP. Under FRS 102, intangible assets always have finite lives and are amortised on a systematic basis over those lives. FRS 102 para 18.21].	Same as old UK GAAP. Intangible assets with finite useful life (including those that are revalued) are amortised. Amortisation is carried out on a systematic basis over the useful lives of the intangible assets. [IAS 38 para 97].

	Old UK GAAP	**New UK GAAP (FRS 102)**	**IFRS**
	The useful economic lives of goodwill and intangible assets are reviewed at the end of each reporting period and revised if necessary. If a useful economic life is revised, the carrying value of the goodwill or intangible asset at the date of revision is amortised over the revised remaining useful economic life. The depreciation method is not required to be reviewed. [FRS 10 para 33].	Similar to old UK GAAP, except that the amortisation period, method and residual value are only reviewed if there is an indication of change since the last reporting date. Changes in the amortisation period/method are accounted for as a change in estimate. [FRS 102 para 18.24]. * See 'Useful life' section above.	Similar to new UK GAAP, except that the amortisation period, method and residual value are reviewed at least once at each annual reporting period. [IAS 38 paras 97, 100, 104].
Intangible assets with indefinite useful life	Intangible assets that are amortised over a period exceeding 20 years from the date of acquisition (or are not amortised) are reviewed for impairment at the end of each reporting period. [FRS 10 para 37].	Not applicable. All intangible assets are considered to have finite lives. [FRS 102 paras 18.19-18.20].	These assets are not amortised. The useful life assessment is reviewed at each annual reporting period to determine whether events and circumstances continue to support an indefinite useful life assessment. Change in the useful life assessment from 'indefinite' to 'finite' is an indicator that an asset might be impaired and is accounted for as a change in estimate. [IAS 38 paras 107, 109, 110]. *FRS 101 RDF (IFRS): Non-amortisation of intangible assets will usually be a departure from the Companies Act 2006 (as updated by SI 2015/980) for the overriding purpose of giving a true and fair view. Disclosure of the departure and its effect are required. [FRS 101 para A2.8A].*
Impairment	In addition to annual impairment reviews for intangible assets with amortisation periods exceeding 20 years, FRS 10 requires an impairment review of all intangible assets at the end of the first full year following their acquisition. [FRS 10 para 34].	Intangible assets are tested for impairment where there is an indication that the asset may be impaired. Existence of impairment indicators is assessed at each reporting date. [FRS 102 paras 18.25, 27.5-27.7].	Same as new UK GAAP. In addition, intangibles with indefinite useful lives are tested for impairment annually, irrespective of whether there is an indication of impairment. [IAS 36 paras 9-10].

Property, plant and equipment (PPE)

	Old UK GAAP	New UK GAAP (FRS 102)	IFRS
Definition	PPE are assets that have physical substance and are held for use in the production or supply of goods or services, for rental to others or for administrative purposes on a continuing basis in the reporting entity's activities. [FRS 15 para 2].	Same as old UK GAAP. [FRS 102 para 17.2]. Biological assets related to agricultural activity, heritage assets, mineral rights and mineral reserves are outside the scoped of section 17. [FRS 102 para 17.3].	Same as old UK GAAP and new UK GAAP. PPE classified as held for sale, biological assets and some others are explicitly outside the scope of IAS 16. [IAS 16 paras 3, 6].
	Residual values are based on prices prevailing at the date of acquisition (or revaluation) and do not take into account expected future price changes. [FRS 15 para 2].	Residual values are based on prices prevailing at the balance sheet date. [FRS 102 Glossary].	Same as new UK GAAP. [IAS 16 para 6].
Initial measurement	PPE is measured initially at cost. [FRS 15 para 6]. Cost includes: • purchase price; • any directly attributable costs to bring the asset to the location and condition necessary for it to be capable of operating in the manner intended by management; and • the initial estimate of costs of dismantling and removing the item and restoring the site on which it is located. There is an accounting policy choice regarding borrowing costs if certain recognition criteria are met. [FRS 15 para 19].	Same as old UK GAAP. [FRS 102 para 17.9]. Borrowing costs may be capitalised where the entity has adopted a policy of capitalising these on qualifying assets. [FRS 102 paras 17.9-17.11, 25.2].	Similar to new UK GAAP, except that borrowing costs that are directly attributable to the acquisition, construction or production of a qualifying asset are required to be capitalised as part of the cost of that asset. [IAS 16 para 16; IAS 23 para 8].
Subsequent measurement	Classes of PPE are carried at cost less accumulated depreciation and any impairment losses. An entity has the option of adopting a policy of revaluation. Where a policy of revaluation is adopted, it is applied to individual classes of tangible fixed assets. [FRS 15 paras 42, 61].	PPE may be carried at either cost less any accumulated amortisation and any accumulated impairment losses (cost model), or revaluation model where PPE is carried at a revalued amount, being its fair value at the date of revaluation, less any accumulated depreciation and subsequent accumulated impairment losses. Where the revaluation model is selected, it is applied to all items of PPE in the same class (that is, having a similar nature, function or use in the business). [FRS 102 paras 17.15, 17.15A, 17.15B].	In addition to the cost model, the revaluation model is an option: classes of PPE are carried at a revalued amount less any accumulated depreciation and subsequent accumulated impairment losses. [IAS 16 paras 29-31].

	Old UK GAAP	New UK GAAP (FRS 102)	IFRS
Revaluation model	Where PPE is subject to a policy of revaluation, its carrying amount should be its current value as at the balance sheet date. FRS 15 does not insist on annual revaluations: the frequency of valuations is supported by detailed guidance in FRS 15. [FRS 15 paras 43, 44, 45-52].	Revaluations should be made with sufficient regularity to ensure that the carrying amount does not differ materially from the fair value at the end of the reporting period. [FRS 102 para 17.15B].	Revaluations should be made with sufficient regularity to ensure that the carrying amount does not differ materially from the fair value at the end of the reporting period. [IAS 16 para 31].
	The following valuation bases may be used for items of PPE that are not impaired: • Non-specialised properties – existing value in use plus acquisition costs. • Specialised properties – depreciated replacement cost. • Properties surplus to an entity's requirements – open market value less selling costs. • Tangible fixed assets other than properties – market value or depreciated replacement cost where market value is not obtainable. [FRS 15 paras 53-59].	The fair value of: • land and buildings is usually determined from market-based evidence by appraisal that is normally undertaken by professionally qualified valuers; and • items of plant and equipment is usually their market value determined by appraisal. [FRS 102 para 17.15C]. If there is no market-based evidence of fair value, because of the specialised nature of the item of PPE and the item is rarely sold (except as part of a continuing business), an entity may estimate fair value using an income or a depreciated replacement cost approach. [FRS 102 para 17.15D].	The fair value of land and buildings is usually determined from market-based evidence. The fair value of plant and equipment is usually market value. Specialised assets are valued using an income-based approach or at depreciated replacement cost. [IAS 16 paras 32, 33].
	Revaluation gains are recognised in the profit and loss account only to the extent (after adjusting for subsequent depreciation) that they reverse revaluation losses previously recognised in the profit and loss account. All other revaluation gains are recognised in the statement of total recognised gains and losses. [FRS 15 para 63].	Revaluation gains are recognised in other comprehensive income and accumulated in equity. However, the gain is recognised in profit or loss to the extent that it reverses a revaluation decrease of the same asset previously recognised in profit or loss. [FRS 102 para 17.15E].	A revaluation gain is recognised in other comprehensive income, unless it reverses a revaluation decrease of the same asset previously recognised in profit or loss. [IAS 16 para 39].
	All revaluation losses that are the result of the consumption of economic benefits should be recognised in the profit and loss account. Otherwise, revaluation losses are recognised as follows: • In the statement of total recognised gains and losses, until the carrying amount falls to depreciated historical cost. • In the profit and loss account for falls in value below depreciated historical cost, except where	Revaluation losses are recognised in other comprehensive income to the extent of any previously recognised revaluation gains accumulated in equity in respect of that asset. If a revaluation loss exceeds the accumulated revaluation gains in respect of that asset, the excess is recognised in profit or loss. [FRS 102 para 17.15F].	Revaluation losses are recognised in profit or loss. However, the loss is recognised in other comprehensive income to the extent of any credit balance existing in the revaluation reserve in respect of that asset. [IAS 16 para 40].

	Old UK GAAP	New UK GAAP (FRS 102)	IFRS
	it can be demonstrated that the recoverable amount is greater than the revalued amount, in which case the fall in value below the recoverable amount is recognised in the statement of total recognised gains and losses. [FRS 15 para 65].		
Major inspection	Some tangible fixed assets require, in addition to routine repairs and maintenance, substantial expenditure every few years for major refits or refurbishment, or the replacement or restoration of major components. For depreciation purposes, an entity accounts separately for major components that have substantially different useful economic lives from the rest of the asset. In such a case, each component is depreciated over its individual useful economic life. Subsequent expenditure incurred in replacing or renewing the component is accounted for as an addition to the tangible fixed asset. The carrying amount of the replaced component is removed from the balance sheet. [FRS 15 para 38].	Same as old UK GAAP. The cost of a major inspection or replacement of parts of an item occurring at regular intervals over its useful life is capitalised to the extent that it meets the recognition criteria of an asset. The carrying amount of the previous inspection or parts replaced is derecognised. [FRS 102 paras 17.6-17.7].	Same as new UK GAAP. [IAS 16 para 13].
Impairment	A review for impairment of a fixed asset or goodwill is carried out if events or changes in circumstances indicate that the carrying amount of the fixed asset or goodwill may not be recoverable. There is no requirement for an impairment review if there are no indicators. [FRS 11 paras 8, 13].	Entities assess if there are any impairment indicators at each reporting date. If there is an indicator, an impairment test is required. [FRS 102 paras 17.24, 27.5].	Same as new UK GAAP. [IAS 16 para 63; IAS 36 para 9].
	No explicit reference to compensation from third parties in FRS 11 or FRS 15.	An entity includes in profit or loss compensation from third parties for items of PPE that were impaired, lost or given up only when the compensation is virtually certain. [FRS 102 para 17.25].	Compensation from third parties for items of PPE that were impaired, lost or given up is included in profit or loss when the compensation becomes receivable. [IAS 16 para 65].
Depreciation – definition	The measure of the cost or revalued amount of the economic benefits of the tangible fixed asset that have been consumed during the period. [FRS 15 para 2].	Same as old UK GAAP. Defined as the systematic allocation of the depreciable amount of an asset over its useful life. [FRS 102 Glossary].	Same as new UK GAAP. [IAS 16 para 6].

	Old UK GAAP	New UK GAAP (FRS 102)	IFRS
Components approach	Where an asset comprises two or more major components with substantially different lives, these assets are depreciated separately over their individual lives. [FRS 15 para 83].	Similar to old UK GAAP. PPE may have significant parts with different useful lives. The cost of an item of PPE is allocated to its significant parts, with each part depreciated separately only when the parts have significantly different patterns of benefit consumption. [FRS 102 para 17.16].	Similar to old UK GAAP and new UK GAAP. PPE may have significant parts with different useful lives. Depreciation is calculated based on each individual part's life. Significant parts that have the same useful life and depreciation method may be grouped in determining the depreciation charge. [IAS 16 paras 43-45].
Depreciation charge	The depreciable amount of a tangible fixed asset is allocated on a systematic basis over its useful economic life. The depreciation method used should reflect as fairly as possible the pattern in which the asset's economic benefits are consumed by the entity.	Same as old UK GAAP. [FRS 102 para 17.19].	Same as old UK GAAP and new UK GAAP. [IAS 16 para 51].
	The depreciation charge for each period is recognised as an expense in the profit and loss account, unless it is permitted to be included in the carrying amount of another asset. [FRS 15 para 77].	Same as old UK GAAP. [FRS 102 para 17.17].	Same as old UK GAAP and new UK GAAP. [IAS 16 para 48].
Depreciable period	The useful economic life of a tangible fixed asset is reviewed at the end of each reporting period and revised if expectations are significantly different from previous estimates. If a useful economic life is revised, the carrying amount of the tangible fixed asset at the date of revision is depreciated over the revised remaining useful economic life. [FRS 15 paras 93, 95].	Similar to old UK GAAP. There is no annual requirement to review the useful economic life, which is only reviewed if an indicator of impairment exists. [FRS 102 paras 17.18-17.19].	Same as old UK GAAP. Similar to new UK GAAP, except that the useful economic life is reviewed annually. [IAS 16 paras 50-51].
Depreciation method	A variety of methods can be used to allocate the depreciable amount of a tangible fixed asset on a systematic basis over its useful economic life. [FRS 15 para 81].	Same as old UK GAAP. The depreciation method should reflect the pattern in which the asset's future economic benefits are expected to be consumed by the entity. [FRS 102 para 17.22].	Same as old UK GAAP and new UK GAAP. [IAS 16 para 60].
	A change in method is only permitted if it results in a fairer presentation. [FRS 15 para 82]. There is no requirement to consider this annually.	The depreciation method is only reviewed if there is an indication that there has been a significant change since the last annual reporting date. [FRS 102 para 17.23].	Similar to new UK GAAP, except that the depreciation method is reviewed annually. [IAS 16 paras 61-62].
	A change in the depreciation method is accounted for as a change in estimate. [FRS 15 para 82].	Same as old UK GAAP. [FRS 102 para 17.23].	Same as old UK GAAP and new UK GAAP. [IAS 16 paras 61-62].

	Old UK GAAP	New UK GAAP (FRS 102)	IFRS
Non-current assets held for sale	Not covered in old UK GAAP. Depreciation continues until the asset is actually disposed of.	A plan to dispose of an asset is an indicator of impairment that triggers the calculation of the asset's recoverable amount for the purpose of determining whether the asset is impaired. [FRS 102 para 17.26]. The asset continues to be depreciated.	PPE is classified as held for sale if its carrying amount will be recovered principally through a sale transaction rather than through continuing use. Assets held for sale, which are not depreciated, are measured at the lower of carrying amount and fair value less costs to sell. [IAS 16 para 3; IFRS 5 paras 6, 15].

Investment property

	Old UK GAAP	New UK GAAP (FRS 102)	IFRS
Definition	An investment property is an interest in land and/or buildings in respect of which construction work and development have been completed, and that is held for its investment potential, with any rental income being negotiated at arm's length.	Similar to old UK GAAP. Investment property is a property (land or building, or part of a building, or both) held by the owner or by a lessee under a finance lease to earn rentals, or for capital appreciation, or both.	Same as new UK GAAP. [IAS 40 para 5].
	Owner-occupied properties (or properties let to and occupied by other group companies) are excluded. [SSAP 19 paras 7(b), 8].	A property interest held for use in the production or supply of goods or services or for administrative purposes is not an investment property. [FRS 102 para 16.2].	Same as new UK GAAP. [IAS 40 para 5].
	The definition of an investment property requires construction work and development to have been completed. FRS 15 applies to assets under construction. [SSAP 19 para 7(a)]	The definition of investment property contains no explicit reference requiring construction work and development to be completed.	Investment property includes property that is being constructed or developed for future use as investment property. [IAS 40 para 8].
Properties occupied by group members	A property that is let to and occupied by another company within an entity's group is not an investment property for the purposes of its individual accounts. [SSAP 19 para 8].	A property that meets the definition of an investment property and is let to and occupied by another company within the entity's group is an investment property in its individual accounts. [FRS 102 para 16.2].	Same as new UK GAAP. [IAS 40 para 5].
Initial measurement	Initial measurement is not referred to in SSAP 19. However, investment properties are included in the balance sheet at their open market value. [SSAP 19 para 11]. Borrowing costs are not mentioned in SSAP 19, but both paragraph 19 of FRS 15 and company law permit capitalisation of borrowing costs. This is an accounting policy choice.	The cost of a purchased investment property is its purchase price plus any directly attributable costs, such as professional fees for legal services, property transfer taxes and other transaction costs. Borrowing costs may be capitalised where the entity has adopted a policy of capitalising borrowing costs. [FRS 102 paras 16.5, 25.2].	Similar to new UK GAAP, except that borrowing costs that are directly attributable to the acquisition, construction or production of a qualifying asset have to be capitalised as part of the cost of that asset. [IAS 40 paras 20-24; IAS 23 paras 10-15].

	Old UK GAAP	New UK GAAP (FRS 102)	IFRS
Subsequent measurement	Investment properties are included in the balance sheet at open market value. [SSAP 19 para 11]. Open market value excludes selling costs (based on RICS PS 4.16). Entities are not permitted to use the cost model – there is no policy choice under SSAP 19.	Investment property is carried at fair value if its fair value can be measured reliably without undue cost or effort. Otherwise, property is classified as property, plant and equipment, and the cost model is applied. [FRS 102 paras 16.7-16.8].	Management may choose as its accounting policy to carry its investment properties at fair value or at cost less depreciation and impairment charges. However, where an investment property is held by a lessee under an operating lease, the entity follows the fair value model for all its investment properties. [IAS 40 paras 30, 34]. Regardless of its policy choice for all other investment property, an entity may choose either the fair value model or the cost model for all investment property – backing liabilities that pay a return linked directly to the fair value of, or returns from, specified assets including that investment property. [IAS 40 para 32A].
Fair value model	Revaluation gains and losses are recognised in the statement of total recognised gains and losses, unless they are permanent deficits (or their reversals). These are recognised in the profit and loss account. [SSAP 19 para 13]. There are exceptions for investment companies, property unit trusts, insurance companies and pension funds. [SSAP 19 paras 13-14].	Gains and losses arising from changes in the fair value of investment property are recognised in profit or loss. [FRS 102 para 16.7].	Same as new UK GAAP. [IAS 40 paras 33-55].
Cost model	The cost model is not permitted under SSAP 19.	Properties carried at cost are accounted for in accordance with section 17's treatment for property, plant and equipment. [FRS 102 para 16.7].	Properties carried at cost follow IAS 16, under which they are carried at cost less accumulated depreciation and any accumulated impairment losses. [IAS 40 para 56].
Transfers	There are no specific rules regarding the transfer of properties to or from investment properties, other than UITF 5, 'Transfers from current to fixed assets'.	If a reliable measure of fair value is no longer available, the property is reclassified as property, plant and equipment. Otherwise, transfer to or from investment properties applies where the property meets or ceases to meet the definition of an investment property. [FRS 102 paras 16.8-16.9].	IAS 40 does not anticipate a situation where fair value is no longer available. IFRS includes further guidance on the situations in which a property is transferred to or from the investment property category (there must be a change in use). [IAS 40 para 57].

Impairment of assets

This section addresses the impairment of assets other than inventories. More detail on the impairment of inventories is included elsewhere in this publication (in the section on inventories).

	Old UK GAAP	New UK GAAP (FRS 102)	IFRS
Definition and scope			
Income-generating unit/ cash– generating unit	Income-generating units (IGUs) are identified by dividing the total income of the entity into as many largely independent income streams as is reasonably practicable. [FRS 11 para 27].	Similar to old UK GAAP, as cash-generating units (CGUs) are comparable to IGUs. A CGU is the smallest identifiable group of assets that generates cash inflows that are largely independent of the cash inflows from other assets or groups of assets. [FRS 102 para 27.8].	Same as new UK GAAP. [IAS 36 para 6].
Scope	FRS 11 applies to fixed assets, so the various current asset categories are not within its scope. FRS 11 also encompasses impairment on investment in subsidiaries, associates and joint ventures.	Assets are subject to an impairment test according to the requirements outlined below, with the following exceptions: • assets arising from construction contracts; • deferred tax assets; • employee benefit assets; • financial assets; • investment property carried at fair value; • biological assets carried at fair value less estimated cost to sell; • deferred acquisition costs; and • intangible assets arising from insurance contracts. [FRS 102 paras 27.1-27.1A].	Wording similar to new UK GAAP. In addition to the assets excluded from the scope of new UK GAAP, IFRS excludes the following assets: • inventories; and • non-current assets classified as held for sale in accordance with IFRS 5. [IAS 36 para 2].
Impairment of assets			
Impairment formula	The impairment review comprises a comparison of the carrying amount of the fixed asset (or IGU, if not reasonably practical to identify cash flows arising from a single fixed asset) with its recoverable amount (the higher of net realisable value and value in use). To the extent that the carrying amount exceeds the recoverable amount,	Similar to old UK GAAP. An asset (or CGU) is impaired when its carrying amount exceeds its recoverable amount (the higher of fair value less costs to sell and its value in use). [FRS 102 paras 27.5, 27.11].	Same as new UK GAAP. [IAS 36 para 8].

	Old UK GAAP	New UK GAAP (FRS 102)	IFRS
	the fixed asset is impaired and is written down. [FRS 11 para 14].		
Impairment losses	Impairments that have been caused by the clear consumption of economic benefits should be charged to the profit and loss account, regardless of whether the asset has been revalued. [FRS 11 para 63].	An impairment loss is recognised immediately in profit and loss, unless the asset is carried at a revalued amount in accordance with another section of FRS 102. Any impairment loss of a revalued asset is treated as a revaluation decrease in accordance with that other section. [FRS 102 para 27.6].	Same as new UK GAAP. [IAS 36 para 60].
Annual assessment of indicators	Goodwill and intangible assets that are amortised over more than 20 years (or not amortised) are reviewed for impairment at the end of each period. [FRS 10 para 37]. A review of other goodwill and intangible assets is required at the end of the first full year after acquisition, and in other periods if events or change in circumstances indicate that the carrying value might not be recoverable. [FRS 10 para 34].	Annual impairment testing is not required.	The following assets are tested annually for impairment, irrespective of whether there is any indication of impairment: • intangible assets with an indefinite useful life or an intangible asset not yet available for use; and • goodwill.
	A review for impairment of a fixed asset or goodwill is carried out if events or changes in circumstances indicate that the carrying amount of the fixed asset or goodwill might not be recoverable. [FRS 11 para 8].	Assets (including goodwill) are tested for impairment where there is an indication that the asset may be impaired. The existence of impairment indicators is assessed at each reporting date. [FRS 102 para 27.7].	Same as new UK GAAP. [IAS 36 paras 9-10, 18].
Indicators of impairment	Impairment occurs because something has happened either to the fixed assets themselves or to the economic environment in which they are operated. It is possible to rely on the use of indicators of impairment to determine when a review for impairment is needed. [FRS 11 para 9]. Examples include: • a current period operating loss in the business; • a significant decline in a fixed asset's market value during the period; • evidence of obsolescence or physical damage to the fixed asset;	Similar indicator approach to old UK GAAP. In addition to the items under FRS 11, further triggers are when the entity's net asset value is above its market capitalisation, or when discount rates change materially. [FRS 102 para 27.9].	Same as new UK GAAP. [IAS 36 para 12].

	Old UK GAAP	New UK GAAP (FRS 102)	IFRS
	• a significant adverse change in the business or the market in which the fixed asset or goodwill is involved; • a significant adverse change in the statutory or other regulatory environment in which the business operates; • a major loss of key employees; • a commitment by management to undertake a significant reorganisation; and • a significant change in interest rates that materially affects the asset's recoverable amount. [FRS 11 para 10].		
Recoverable amount	Recoverable amount is the higher of net realisable value and value in use. [FRS 11 para 2].	Similar to old UK GAAP, although the terminology is different. 'Recoverable amount' is the higher of an asset's (or CGU's) fair value less costs to sell and its value in use. [FRS 102 paras 27.11-27.13].	Same as new UK GAAP (although IAS 36 now uses the terminology 'fair value less costs of disposal'). [IAS 36 para 6].
Value in use	The value in use is the present value of the future cash flows obtainable as a result of an asset's continued use, including those resulting from its ultimate disposal. [FRS 11 para 2]. The value in use of a fixed asset is estimated individually, where reasonably practicable. Where it is not reasonably practicable to identify cash flows arising from an individual fixed asset, value in use is calculated at the level of IGUs.	Similar to old UK GAAP. The value in use is defined as the present value of the future cash flows expected to be derived from an asset or CGU. Future cash flows are estimated for the asset in its current condition. Cash inflows or outflows from financing activities and income tax receipts or payments are not included. [FRS 102 paras 27.15-27.20].	Same as new UK GAAP, but there is more extensive guidance about future cash flows estimation. [IAS 36 paras 30-53].
Net realisable value/Fair value less costs to sell/Fair value less costs of disposal	The net realisable value is the amount at which an asset could be disposed of, less any direct selling costs. [FRS 11 para 2]. The net realisable value of an asset that is traded on an active market is based on market value. [FRS 11 para 22]. Examples of direct selling costs are legal costs and stamp duty. Any costs relating to the removal of a	Similar to old UK GAAP. Fair value less costs to sell is estimated based on a hierarchy of reliability of evidence, of: • a price in a binding sale agreement in an arm's length transaction or market price in an active market, less costs of disposal; and • best available information to reflect the amount that an entity could obtain at the reporting date from disposal of the asset in an arm's length transaction between	Fair value measurement estimates the price at which an orderly transaction to sell the asset would take place between market participants at the measurement date under current market conditions. Where a price for an identical asset is not observable, an entity measures fair value using another valuation technique that maximises the use of relevant observable inputs and minimises the use of unobservable inputs – using the assumptions that market participants would use

	Old UK GAAP	New UK GAAP (FRS 102)	IFRS
	sitting tenant are also direct selling costs of a building. [FRS 11 para 23].	knowledgeable, willing parties, less costs of disposal. Recent transactions for similar assets within the same industry need to be considered. [FRS 102 para 27.14].	when pricing the asset or liability, including assumptions about risk. [IFRS 13 paras 2, 3].
Allocation of goodwill	Capitalised goodwill is allocated to IGUs or groups of similar units. [FRS 11 para 34]. FRS 11 does not specify which IGUs goodwill should be allocated to.	Goodwill is allocated to the CGUs that are expected to benefit from the synergies of the combination. If such allocation is not possible and the reporting entity has not integrated the acquired business, the acquired entity is measured as a whole when testing goodwill for impairment. If such allocation is not possible and the acquired business has been integrated, the entire group is considered when testing goodwill for impairment. [FRS 102 para 27.27].	Goodwill acquired in a business combination is allocated to the CGUs that are expected to benefit from the synergies of the combination. IAS 36 includes comprehensive guidance on how to allocate goodwill for a range of different circumstances. Goodwill is tested for impairment at the lowest level at which it is monitored by management. CGUs may be grouped for testing, but the grouping cannot be higher than an operating segment as defined in IFRS 8 (before aggregation). [IAS 36 paras 80-87].
Allocation of impairment losses	In the absence of an obvious impairment of specific assets within an IGU, the impairment should be allocated: • first, to any goodwill in the unit; • thereafter, to any capitalised intangible asset in the unit; and • finally, to the tangible assets in the unit, on a pro rata or more appropriate basis.	An impairment loss is allocated to reduce the carrying amount of the CGU's assets, as follows: • first, to reduce the carrying amount of any goodwill allocated to the CGU; and • then, to the other assets of the unit pro rata on the basis of the carrying amount of each asset in the CGU.	Same as new UK GAAP. [IAS 36 paras 104-105].
	An intangible asset with a readily ascertainable market value should not be written down below its net realisable value. A tangible asset should not be written down below a net realisable value that can be measured reliably. [FRS 11 paras 48, 49].	The carrying amounts of an asset should not be reduced below the highest of: • fair value less costs to sell; • value in use; and • zero. Any impairment loss that cannot be allocated to an asset is allocated to the other assets of the unit pro rata on the basis of the carrying amount of those other assets. [FRS 102 paras 27.21-27.23].	

	Old UK GAAP	New UK GAAP (FRS 102)	IFRS
Reversal of impairment	Impairment losses on goodwill and intangible fixed assets are reversed if there is an external event reversing the impairment in an unforeseen way or the loss arose on an intangible with a readily ascertainable market value. [FRS 11 para 60]. However, this is extremely rare and difficult to demonstrate in practice. If the recoverable amount of a tangible fixed asset or investment increases because of a change in economic conditions or in the expected use of the asset, the resulting reversal of the impairment loss is recognised in the current period to the extent that it increases the carrying amount of the fixed asset up to the amount that it would have been if the original impairment had not occurred. [FRS 11 para 56].	Impairment losses on all assets (excluding goodwill when the relevant change in legislation and FRS 102 applies) are reversed if the reasons for the impairment loss have ceased to apply. At each reporting date after recognition of the impairment loss, an entity assesses whether there is any indication that an impairment loss may have decreased or may no longer exist. This assessment will depend on whether the prior impairment loss was based on the recoverable amount of an individual asset or the recoverable amount of a CGU. Broadly, the impairment loss is reversed if the recoverable amount of an asset or CGU exceeds its carrying amount. The amount of the reversal is subject to certain limitations. [FRS 102 paras 27.28-27.31].	Similar to new UK GAAP. IFRS includes more detailed guidance on assessing if an impairment loss has reversed, and also on reversal of impairment for an individual asset, a CGU and goodwill. [IAS 36 paras 109-125].

Leases

	Old UK GAAP	New UK GAAP (FRS 102)	IFRS
Definition and scope			
Definition	A lease is a contract between a lessor and a lessee for the hire of a specific asset. The lessor retains ownership of the asset but conveys the right to use the asset to the lessee for an agreed period of time in return for the payment of specified rentals. The term 'lease', as used in this statement, also applies to other arrangements in which one party retains ownership of an asset but conveys the right to the use of the asset to another party for an agreed period of time in return for specified payments. [SSAP 21 para 14].	A lease is an agreement whereby the lessor conveys to the lessee, in return for a payment or a series of payments, the right to use an asset for an agreed period of time. [FRS 102 Glossary]. Arrangements that do not take the legal form of a lease – but that convey rights to use assets in return for payments – are, in substance, leases and are accounted as such. Determining whether an arrangement is, or contains, a lease is based on the arrangement's substance and requires an assessment of whether: • fulfilment of the arrangement is dependent on the use of a specific asset or assets; and	Same as new UK GAAP. [IAS 17 para 4; IFRIC 4 para 6].

	Old UK GAAP	New UK GAAP (FRS 102)	IFRS
		• the arrangement conveys a right to use the asset. [FRS 102 paras 20.3-20.3A].	
Scope of the standard	SSAP 21 does not apply to lease contracts concerning: • the rights to explore for or to exploit natural resources, such as oil, gas, timber, metals and other minerals ; and • licensing agreements for items such as motion picture films, video recordings, plays, manuscripts, patents and copyrights.	The section on leases applies to accounting for all leases other than: • leases to explore for or use minerals, oil, natural gas and similar non-regenerative resources; • licensing agreements for such items as motion picture films, video recordings, plays, manuscripts, patents and copyrights; • measurement of property held by lessees that is accounted for as investment property and measurement of investment property provided by lessors under operating leases; • measurement of biological assets held by lessees under finance leases and biological assets provided by lessors under operating leases; and • leases that could lead to a loss for the lessor or the lessee as a result of non-typical contractual terms. [FRS 102 para 20.1].	Same as new UK GAAP. [IAS 17 para 2; IAS 37 para 5].
Lease classification			
General characteristics	Leases are classified into finance leases and operating leases. The distinction between a finance lease and an operating lease is usually evident from the terms of the contract between the lessor and the lessee. A finance lease is a lease that transfers substantially all the risks and rewards of ownership of an asset to the lessee. [SSAP 21 para 15].	A lease is classified at inception as a finance lease if it transfers to the lessee substantially all the risks and rewards incidental to ownership. All other leases are treated as operating leases. Whether a lease is a finance lease or an operating lease depends on the substance of the transaction rather than the form of the contract. [FRS 102 paras 20.4-20.5].	Same as new UK GAAP. [IAS 17 paras 8, 10].
Examples of situations that would normally lead to a lease being classified as a finance lease	SSAP 21 presumes that a transfer of risks and rewards occurs if, at the inception of the lease, the present value of the minimum lease payments amounts to substantially all (normally 90% or more) of the fair value of the leased asset.	Examples of situations that (individually or in combination) would normally lead to a lease being classified as a finance lease are:	Same as new UK GAAP. [IAS 17 para 10].

	Old UK GAAP	New UK GAAP (FRS 102)	IFRS
	However, this presumption can be rebutted. [SSAP 21 paras 15-16]. SSAP 21 does not provide additional guidance on lease classification in the standard. However, there are extensive guidance notes.	• the lease transfers ownership of the asset to the lessee by the end of the lease term; • the lessee has the option to purchase the asset at a price that is expected to be sufficiently lower than the fair value at the date the option becomes exercisable for it to be reasonably certain, at the inception of the lease, that the option will be exercised; • the lease term is for the major part of the economic life of the asset, even if title is not transferred; • at the inception of the lease, the present value of the minimum lease payments amounts to at least substantially all of the fair value of the leased asset; and • the leased assets are of such a specialised nature that only the lessee can use them without major modifications. [FRS 102 para 20.5]. The similarity of the definitions means that, in practice, a lease that is classified as a finance lease under SSAP 21 would, in most cases, be classed as a finance lease under FRS 102.	
Sale and lease back transactions	*Sale and finance leaseback* Where the transaction is a sale and leaseback, but the substance is that of a financing, any apparent profit or loss should be deferred and amortised over the shorter of the lease term and the useful life of the asset, and no adjustment is made to the carrying value of the asset [SSAP 21 para 46].	*Sale and finance leaseback* For sale and lease back transactions resulting in a lease back of a finance lease, any gain realised by the seller-lessee on the transaction is deferred and amortised through profit or loss over the lease term. [FRS 102 para 20.33].	Same as new UK GAAP. [IAS 17 para 59].
	Sale and operating leaseback If a sale and leaseback transaction results in an operating lease, and it is clear that the transaction is established at fair value, any profit or loss is recognised immediately. [SSAP 21 para 47(a)]. If the sale price is below fair value, any profit or loss is recognised immediately; except that, if the	*Sale and operating leaseback* If a sale and leaseback transaction results in an operating lease, and it is clear that the transaction is established at fair value, the seller-lessee recognises any profit or loss immediately. If the sale price is below fair value, the seller-lessee recognises any profit or loss immediately, unless	Same as new UK GAAP. [IAS 17 paras 61, 63, IG].

	Old UK GAAP	New UK GAAP (FRS 102)	IFRS
	apparent loss is compensated by future rentals at below market price, it should (to that extent) be deferred and amortised over the remainder of the lease term or, if shorter, the period during which the reduced rentals are chargeable. [SSAP 21 para 47(b)]. If the sale price is above fair value, the excess over fair value is deferred and amortised over the shorter of the lease term and the period to the next rent review. [SSAP 21 para 47(c)].	the loss is compensated for by future lease payments at below market price. In that case, the seller-lessee defers and amortises such loss in proportion to the lease payments over the period for which the asset is expected to be used. If the sale price is above fair value, the seller-lessee defers the excess over fair value and amortises it over the period for which the asset is expected to be used. [FRS 102 para 20.34].	
Lease incentives	All incentives for the agreement of a new or renewed operating lease are recognised as an integral part of the net payment agreed for the use of the leased asset, irrespective of the incentive's nature or form or the timing of payments. A lessee recognises the aggregate benefit of incentives as a reduction of rental expense. The benefit is allocated over the shorter of the lease term and a period ending on a date from which it is expected that the prevailing market rental will be payable. [UITF 28 paras 13 –15].	The aggregate benefit of incentives is recognised as a reduction of rental expense over the lease term (market rent reviews are ignored) on a straight-line basis, unless another systematic basis is representative of the time pattern of the benefit of the leased asset. [FRS 102 para 20.15A].	Same as new UK GAAP. [SIC 15 paras 3-5].
Leases of land and buildings	There are no detailed rules regarding the allocation between the land and buildings elements of a lease.	Similar to old UK GAAP, there are no detailed rules regarding the allocation between the land and buildings elements of a lease.	Assessment of each element of a lease for both land and buildings is required to determine classification of each element as a finance lease or operating lease.
Lease treatment in the financial statements of a lessee			
Finance lease	Initial recognition of finance leases is at the present value of the minimum lease payments, derived by discounting them at the interest rate implicit in the lease. [SSAP 21 para 32]. However, where the fair value of the asset is a sufficiently close approximation to the present value of the minimum lease payments, the fair value may be used instead. [SSAP 21 para 33]. An asset leased under a finance lease is depreciated over the shorter of the lease term and	Similar to old UK GAAP. The assets and liabilities are recognised at fair value or, if lower, at the present value of the minimum lease payments at the inception of the lease. This is determined by discounting the minimum lease payments using the interest rate implicit in the lease. Subsequent measurement: assets are depreciated in accordance with section 17 of the standard (Property, plant and equipment), or over the lease term if shorter. The lessee apportions minimum	Same as new UK GAAP. [IAS 17 paras 20, 25, 27].

	Old UK GAAP	New UK GAAP (FRS 102)	IFRS
	its useful life. However, in the case of a hire purchase contract that has the characteristics of a finance lease, the asset is depreciated over its useful life. [SSAP 21 para 36].	lease payments between finance charge and reduction of outstanding liability. [FRS 102 paras 20.9-20.12].	
Operating lease	Payments under operating leases are recognised as an expense on a straight-line basis over the lease term, unless another systematic basis is more representative of the time pattern of the user's benefit. [SSAP 21 para 37].	Similar to old UK GAAP. The rental payments are recorded as an expense on a straight-line basis over the lease term, unless another systematic basis is representative of the time pattern of the user's benefit, or the payments to the lessor are structured to increase in line with expected inflation to compensate for the lessor's expected cost increases. [FRS 102 para 20.15].	Same as old UK GAAP, and similar to new UK GAAP, except for the expected inflation adjustments. [IAS 17 para 33].
Lease treatment in the financial statements of a lessor			
Finance lease	The amount due from the lessee under a finance lease is recorded in the balance sheet of a lessor as a debtor at the amount of the net investment in the lease, after making provisions for items such as bad and doubtful rentals receivable. [SSAP 21 para 38].	Assets held under a finance lease are recognised and presented as a receivable at an amount equal to the net investment in the lease. [FRS 102 para 20.17].	Same as new UK GAAP. [IAS 17 para 36].
	Total gross earnings under a finance lease are required to be allocated to accounting periods, to give a constant rate of return on the lessor's net cash investment in the lease. [SSAP 21 para 39].	The recognition of finance income is an area of major difference between old UK GAAP and FRS 102. A constant rate of return on the net investment in the lease, rather than the net cash investment, is required. [FRS 102 para 20.19].	Same as new UK GAAP. [IAS 17 para 39].
	The net cash investment represents the total cash invested, after taking into account all of the cash flows associated with the lease. It differs, therefore, from the amount of the net investment in the lease, as it takes account of other cash flows (such as tax).		
Operating lease	Assets held for use in operating leases are recorded as a fixed asset and depreciated over their useful economic life. [SSAP 21 para 42]. Rental income from an operating lease (excluding charges for services such as insurance and maintenance) is recognised on a straight-line basis over the period of the lease, even if the payments	Similar to old UK GAAP. Recognition of income is the same as old UK GAAP, except that the straight-line basis is not required where the payments to the lessor are structured to increase in line with expected inflation to compensate for the lessor's expected inflationary cost increases. [FRS 102 para 20.25].	Similar to new UK GAAP, except for the expected inflation adjustments. [IAS 17 paras 50-51, 53].

	Old UK GAAP	New UK GAAP (FRS 102)	IFRS
	are not made on such a basis, unless another systematic and rational basis is more representative of the time pattern in which the benefit from the leased asset is receivable. [SSAP 21 para 43].		

Inventories

	Old UK GAAP	New UK GAAP (FRS 102)	IFRS
Definition and scope			
Definition	Stocks include goods purchased for resale, consumable stores, raw materials, work in progress, long-term contract balances and finished goods. [SSAP 9 para 16].	Inventories are assets: • held for sale in the ordinary course of business; • in the process of production for such sale; or • in the form of materials or supplies to be consumed in the production process or in the rendering of services. [FRS 102 para 13.1].	Same as new UK GAAP. [IAS 2 para 6].
Scope of the standard	There is no list of items excluded from scope.	Section 13 does not apply to the following assets, which are covered by other sections: • work in progress under construction contracts; • financial instruments; • biological assets related to agricultural activity; and • agricultural produce at the point of harvest. [FRS 102 para 13.2].	Same as new UK GAAP. [IAS 2 paras 2-3].
		Other than the disclosure requirements, section 13 does not apply to inventories measured at fair value less costs to sell through profit or loss at each reporting date. The July 2015 amendments to FRS 102, clarify that inventories are not measured at fair value less costs to sell unless it is a more relevant measure of the entity's performance because the entity operates in an active market where sale can be	IAS 2 does not apply to the measurement of inventories held by: • producers of agricultural and forest products, agricultural produce after harvest, and minerals and mineral products, to the extent that they are measured at net realisable value in accordance with well-established practices in those industries.

	Old UK GAAP	New UK GAAP (FRS 102)	IFRS
		achieved at published prices, and inventory is a store of readily realisable value. [FRS 102 para 13.3].	• commodity broker-traders who measure their inventories at fair value less costs to sell. The inventories referred to are principally acquired with the purpose of selling in the near future and generating a profit from fluctuations in price or broker-traders' margin. [IAS 2 paras 3, 5].
Measurement and impairment	Inventories are initially recognised at cost, which includes all costs of purchase, costs of conversion and other costs incurred in bringing the inventories to their present location and condition. Stocks are stated at the total of the lower of cost and net realisable value of the separate items of stock or of groups of similar items. [SSAP 9 para 26]. The comparison of cost and net realisable value is made in respect of each item of stock separately. Where this is impracticable, groups or categories of similar stock may be taken together. Comparing the total realisable value of stocks with the total cost could result in an unacceptable setting-off of foreseeable losses against unrealised profits. [SSAP 9 para 2]. Net realisable value is the actual or estimated selling price (net of trade but before settlement discounts) less all further costs to completion and all costs to be incurred in marketing, selling and distribution. [SSAP 9 para 21].	Same as old UK GAAP, although the phrase 'net realisable value' is not used. Instead, FRS 102 uses the phrase 'estimated selling price less costs to complete and sell'. This is synonymous with 'net realisable value'. [FRS 102 paras 13.4-13.5, section 27]. Inventories held for distribution at no or nominal consideration are measured at cost, adjusted, where applicable, for any loss of service potential. (Measurement is at the lower of this amount and replacement cost, under the July 2015 amendments.) [FRS 102 para 13.4A]. If an item of inventory (or group of similar items) is impaired, the entity should measure the inventory (or the group) at its selling price less costs to complete and sell, and recognise the irrecoverable carrying amount as an impairment loss immediately in profit or loss. [FRS 102 para 13.19]. Section 27 of FRS 102 contains specific requirements for measuring impairment of inventory.	Same as old UK GAAP and new UK GAAP. However, IAS 2 refers to 'net realisable value' and it does not have specific guidance for inventories held for distribution at no or nominal consideration. [IAS 2 paras 9-10, 28-33]. IAS 2 does not refer to impairments of inventory. However, it has guidance for inventory write-downs which are taken directly to expense in the period in which they occur. [IAS 2 para 34]. IAS 36 on impairment does not apply to inventories.
Cost of inventories			
Costs of purchase	Costs of purchase comprise purchase price including import duties, transport and handling costs and any other directly attributable costs, less trade discounts, rebates and subsidies. [SSAP 9 para 18].	Same as old UK GAAP. [FRS 102 para 13.6]. Where inventories are acquired through non-exchange transactions, cost is measured at fair value as at the date of acquisition. [FRS 102 para 13.5A].	Same as new UK GAAP, except that IFRS does not have specific guidance for inventories acquired through non-exchange transactions. [IAS 2 para 11].

	Old UK GAAP	New UK GAAP (FRS 102)	IFRS
Costs of conversion	'Costs of conversion' comprise: • costs that are specifically attributable to units of production – for example, direct labour, direct expenses and sub-contracted work; • production overheads and other overheads, if any, attributable in the particular circumstances of the business to bringing the product or service to its present location and condition. [SSAP 9 paras 19-20].	Same as old UK GAAP. [FRS 102 para 13.8].	Same as new UK GAAP. [IAS 2 para 12].
Borrowing costs	Borrowing costs are not explicitly addressed in SSAP 9. Consistent with fixed assets, practice is to either expense such costs or capitalise within stock.	An entity can adopt a policy of capitalising borrowing costs that are directly attributable to the construction or production of a qualifying asset. This includes inventories that take a substantial period of time to produce. However, the financing costs of inventories purchased on deferred settlement terms are recognised as an expense, unless the inventory is a qualifying asset under section 25 of FRS 102 and the entity adopts a policy of capitalising borrowing costs. [FRS 102 paras 13.7, 25.2].	Borrowing costs meeting specific criteria are included in the cost of inventories as identified by IAS 23. [IAS 2 para 17].
Cost formulas	Common costing methods include first-in, first-out (FIFO) and weighted average cost. Methods such as base stock and last-in, first-out (LIFO) are not appropriate. [SSAP 9 App 1 para 12]. Management exercises judgement to ensure that the method chosen to allocate costs to stocks provides the fairest possible approximation to cost. [SSAP 9 para 4, App 1 para 12]. Use of the same cost formula for all similar stocks is not specified, but consistency is a fundamental principle.	Similar to old UK GAAP, but explicit that the same cost formula is used for all inventories that have a similar nature and use to the entity. The cost of inventories used is determined by using either the FIFO or weighted average cost formula. LIFO is not permitted. [FRS 102 paras 13.17-13.18].	Same as new UK GAAP. [IAS 2 para 25].
Techniques for measuring cost	An entity may use techniques for measuring the cost of stock that, in management's judgement, provide the fairest practicable approximation to cost. [SSAP 9 App 1 paras 11-12]. The retail method, which measures cost by reducing selling price by an estimated profit	An entity may use techniques for measuring the cost of inventories if the results approximate to cost. Accepted techniques, if the result approximates to cost, are: • standard cost method; • retail method; and	Similar to new UK GAAP, although the most recent purchase price is not mentioned as an example. [IAS 2 para 21].

	Old UK GAAP	New UK GAAP (FRS 102)	IFRS
	margin, is acceptable only if the result is a reasonable approximation to cost. [SSAP 9 App 1 para 14]. The most recent purchase price is specifically prohibited. [SSAP 9 App 1 para 13].	• most recent purchase price. [FRS 102 para 13.16].	
Joint products and by-products	Where the cost of minor by-products is not separable from the cost of the principal products, stocks of such by-products may be stated in accounts at their net realisable value. In this case, the costs of the main products are calculated after deducting the net realisable value of the by-products. [SSAP 9 App 1 para 15].	For joints products, the cost of the raw materials is allocated between the products on a rational and consistent basis. By-products (where immaterial) are measured at selling price less costs to complete and sell; this amount is then deducted from the cost of the main product. [FRS 102 para 13.10].	Same as new UK GAAP. [IAS 2 para 14].

Provisions and contingencies

	Old UK GAAP	New UK GAAP (FRS 102)	IFRS
Definition and scope			
Definition	A provision is a liability of uncertain timing or amount. [FRS 12 para 2].	Same as old UK GAAP. [FRS 102 para 21.1].	Same as new UK GAAP. [IAS 37 para 10].
Scope of the standard	FRS 12 does not apply to: • financial instruments that are carried at fair value; • executory contracts, except where the contract is onerous; • insurance contracts with policy-holders in insurance entities; • provisions dealt with by other standards; • leases, unless they are onerous; • pension costs; • deferred taxes; or • long-term contracts. [FRS 12 paras 3, 8]. Additionally, for companies not applying FRS 26, FRS 12 excludes financial instruments that are	Similar to old UK GAAP. Financial guarantee contracts are included in the scope of the section for provisions in FRS 102 unless the entity has chosen to apply IAS 39 and/or IFRS 9, or has elected under FRS 103 to continue the application of insurance contract accounting. [FRS 102 paras 21.1 – 21.2].	Similar to new UK GAAP. Financial instruments (including guarantees) dealt with under IAS 39 are excluded from the scope of IAS 37. [IAS 37 para 1].

	Old UK GAAP	New UK GAAP (FRS 102)	IFRS
	not carried at fair value (these instruments are accounted for using FRS 4 requirements). For companies applying FRS 26, FRS 12 does not apply to financial instruments (including guarantees) that are within FRS 26's scope. [FRS 12 para 5].		
Provisions			
Recognition	A provision is recognised when: • an entity has a present obligation (legal or constructive) as a result of a past event; • it is probable that a transfer of economic benefits will be required to settle the obligation; and • a reliable estimate can be made of the amount of the obligation. [FRS 12 para 14]. A present obligation arising from a past event may take the form either of a legal obligation or of a constructive obligation. An obligating event leaves the entity no realistic alternative to settling the obligation. If the entity can avoid the future expenditure by its future actions, it has no present obligation, and no provision is required. [FRS 12 paras 17-19].	Same as old UK GAAP. [FRS 102 para 21.4].	Same as new UK GAAP. [IAS 37 paras 14-26].
Initial measurement	The amount recognised as a provision is the best estimate of the amount required to settle the obligation at the reporting date. Where material, the amount of the provision is the present value of the amount expected to be required to settle the obligation. [FRS 12 para 36].	Same as old UK GAAP. [FRS 102 para 21.7].	Same as new UK GAAP. [IAS 37 paras 36, 45].
Reimbursement	Where some or all of the amount required to settle a provision is to be reimbursed by another party, management recognises the reimbursement as a separate asset only when it is virtually certain that it will receive the reimbursement on settlement of the obligation. The reimbursement receivable is presented on the balance sheet as an asset; it is not offset against the provision. The amount of any expected reimbursement is disclosed. Net	Same as old UK GAAP. [FRS 102 para 21.9].	Same as new UK GAAP. [IAS 37 paras 53-58].

	Old UK GAAP	New UK GAAP (FRS 102)	IFRS
	presentation is permitted in the profit and loss account. [FRS 12 para 56].		
Subsequent measurement	Provisions are reviewed at each balance sheet date and adjusted to reflect the current best estimate. If it is no longer probable that a transfer of economic benefits will be required to settle the obligation, the provision is reversed. [FRS 12 para 62].	Same as old UK GAAP. [FRS 102 paras 21.10-21.11].	Same as new UK GAAP. [IAS 37 paras 59-60].
Contingencies			
Contingent liabilities	Contingent liabilities are either: • possible obligations for which it has yet to be confirmed whether the entity has an obligation that could lead to a transfer of economic benefits; or • present obligations that do not meet the recognition criteria because either it is not probable that a transfer of economic benefits will be required to settle the obligation, or a sufficiently reliable estimate of the amount of the obligation cannot be made. [FRS 12 para 2]. A contingent liability is disclosed, unless the possibility of a transfer of economic benefits is remote. [FRS 12 para 28].	Same as old UK GAAP. [FRS 102 paras 21.12, 21.15].	Same as new UK GAAP. [IAS 37 paras 10, 27-28; IFRS 3 para 23].
Contingent assets	An entity does not recognise a contingent asset. [FRS 12 para 31]. However, where the realisation of the profit is virtually certain, the related asset is not a contingent asset, and it should be recognised. A contingent asset is disclosed where an inflow of economic benefits is probable. [FRS 12 para 34].	Same as old UK GAAP. [FRS 102 paras 21.13, 21.16].	Same as new UK GAAP. [IAS 37 paras 10, 31, 33].
Prejudicial disclosures	In extremely rare cases, disclosure of some or all of the information required by the standard can be expected to prejudice seriously the position of the entity in a dispute with other parties. In such cases an entity need not disclose the information,	There is an exemption where disclosure can be expected to prejudice seriously the position of the entity in a dispute with other parties, but this has been revised in the July 2015 amendments to	Similar to old UK GAAP, but there is no reference to disclosure required by law. [IAS 37 para 92].

	Old UK GAAP	New UK GAAP (FRS 102)	IFRS
	unless its disclosure is required by law, but should disclose the general nature of the dispute, together with the fact that, and reason why, the information has not been disclosed. [FRS 12 para 97].	FRS 102 to require some minimum disclosures. [FRS 102 para 21.17].	*FRS 101 RDF (IFRS): In the July 2015 amendments to FRS 101, the 'seriously prejudicial' exemption in IAS 37 is amended to require some minimum disclosures. [FRS 101 para AG1(s)].*

Events after the end of the reporting period

FRS 21 is a converged standard that mirrors IAS 10.

	Old UK GAAP	New UK GAAP (FRS 102)	IFRS
Definitions			
Events after the end of the reporting period	Events after the end of the reporting period are those events, favourable and unfavourable, that occur between the end of the reporting period and the date when the financial statements are authorised for issue. [FRS 21 para 3].	Same as old UK GAAP. [FRS 102 para 32.2].	Same as new UK GAAP. [IAS 10 para 3].
Adjusting event	Adjusting events provide further evidence of conditions that existed at the end of the reporting period and lead to adjustments to the financial statements. [FRS 21 paras 3, 8].	Same as old UK GAAP. [FRS 102 paras 32.2(a), 32.5].	Same as new UK GAAP. [IAS 10 para 3(a)].
Non-adjusting event	Non-adjusting events relate to conditions that arose after the end of the reporting period and do not lead to adjustments, only to disclosures in the financial statements. [FRS 21 paras 3, 10].	Same as old UK GAAP. [FRS 102 paras 32.2(b), 32.7].	Same as new UK GAAP. [IAS 10 para 3(b)].
Recognition and measurement			
Dividends	Dividends proposed or declared after the end of the reporting period are not recognised as a liability in the reporting period. [FRS 21 paras 12, 13; FRS 25 AG13].	Same as old UK GAAP. [FRS 102 para 32.8].	Same as new UK GAAP. [IAS 10 paras 12-13].
Date of authorisation for issue	Management discloses the date on which the financial statements were authorised for issue and who gave that authorisation. If the owners or other persons have the power to amend the financial statements after issue, this fact is also disclosed. [FRS 21 para 17].	Same as old UK GAAP. [FRS 102 para 32.9].	Same as new UK GAAP. [IAS 10 paras 4-6].

Equity

FRS 102 includes a separate section on equity. There is no discrete accounting standard under IFRS and old UK GAAP dealing with accounting for equity instruments; equity instruments are addressed in various standards. Equity-settled share-based payment transactions are discussed in the 'Income and expenses' section of this publication.

	Old UK GAAP	New UK GAAP (FRS 102)	IFRS
Definitions			
Issue of equity shares	Old UK GAAP is not explicit. In practice, equity instruments are initially recognised at the fair value of the consideration received, except where legal reliefs or exemptions that allow for a different measurement basis are used.	Equity instruments are measured at the fair value of the cash or other resources received or receivable, net of direct issue costs. [FRS 102 para 22.8] If the entity receives the cash or other resources before equity instruments are issued, and the entity cannot be required to repay the cash or other resources received, the entity recognises the corresponding increase in equity. [FRS 102 para 22.7].	IFRS is not explicit, but the application is, in practice, the same as new UK GAAP.
Puttable financial instruments and obligations arising on liquidation	Puttable financial instruments (and instruments that impose on the entity an obligation to deliver a pro rata share in net assets only on liquidation) are classified as equity if specified criteria are met. [FRS 25 paras 16A-16D].	Similar to old UK GAAP. [FRS 102 para 22.4].	Same as old UK GAAP. [IAS 32 paras 16A-16D].
Compound financial instruments	The issuer of a compound financial instrument (such as convertible debt) evaluates the terms of the instrument and classifies liability and equity components separately. This classification is not subsequently revised. [FRS 25 paras 28-30].	Same as old UK GAAP. [FRS 102 paras 22.13-22.14].	Same as old UK GAAP. [IAS 32 paras 28-30].
Converting compound instruments at or before maturity	On conversion of a convertible instrument at maturity, the entity derecognises the liability component and recognises it as equity. The original equity component remains as equity (although it may be transferred from one line item within equity to another). There is no gain or loss on conversion at maturity. [FRS 25 para AG32].	There is no specific guidance. In our view, the guidance under old UK GAAP and IAS 32 should be applied.	Same as old UK GAAP. [IAS 32 para AG32].
Settling debt instruments with shares ('Debt for equity swaps')	No specific guidance. In our view there is an accounting policy choice. One option is that these transactions should be accounted for in the same	No specific guidance but FRS 102 is clear that an entity should measure equity instruments issued to settle the liability 'at the fair value of the cash or other resources received or receivable'.	A gain or loss to be recognised in profit or loss when a financial liability is settled through the issuance of the entity's own equity instruments. The amount of the gain or loss recognised in

	Old UK GAAP	New UK GAAP (FRS 102)	IFRS
	way as when convertible debt is converted into shares. The other option is that the debt that has been extinguished may be viewed as having been repurchased, with the equity instruments being the consideration for the repurchase. Entities applying FRS 26 will also apply UITF 47 (IFRIC 19). UITF 47 requires equity instruments issued for the extinguishment of debt to be recognised at their fair value. For entities not applying FRS 26, FRS 4 requires new debt instruments to be recognised at the net proceeds, that is, the fair value of the consideration received. The consideration for the equity instruments is relief from the debt cancelled in exchange for the equity issued. The equity instruments issued could, therefore, be recognised at the fair value of the debt cancelled. This choice should be applied consistently.	Accordingly, the entity records the equity instruments at the fair value of the debt extinguished. [FRS 102 para 22.8]. The difference is recorded in profit or loss.	profit or loss is the difference between the carrying value of the financial liability (or part of a financial liability) extinguished and the fair value of the equity instruments issued. [IFRS 19 para 6].
Treasury shares	If an entity reacquires its own equity instruments, those instruments are 'treasury shares', and the consideration paid is deducted from equity. No gain or loss is recognised in profit or loss on the purchase, sale, issue or cancellation of an entity's own equity instruments. [FRS 25 para 33].	Same as old UK GAAP. [FRS 102 para 22.16].	Same as old UK GAAP. [IAS 32 para 33].
Minority interest /non-controlling interest	The consolidated balance sheet shows separately the aggregate of the capital and reserves attributable to minority interests. [FRS 2 para 35].	Same as old UK GAAP. In consolidated financial statements, any non-controlling interest in the net assets of a subsidiary is included in equity separately from the equity of owners of the parent. [FRS 102 para 22.19].	Same as old UK GAAP. [IFRS 10 para 10].

4. Consolidated and separate financial statements

Consolidation

For entities reporting under IFRS, the IFRS column below refers to both IAS 27 'Separate financial statements' and IFRS 10 'Consolidated financial statements'.

	Old UK GAAP	New UK GAAP (FRS 102)	IFRS (IFRS 10 and IAS 27)
Definitions			
Control	Control is the ability of an undertaking to direct the financial and operating policies of another undertaking with a view to gaining economic benefits from its activities. [FRS 2 para 6].	Same as old UK GAAP. Control is the power to govern the financial and operating policies of an entity to obtain benefits from its activities. [FRS 102 para 9.4].	An investor controls an investee only if the investor has all of the following: • power over the investee; • exposure, or rights, to variable returns from its involvement with the investee; and • the ability to use its power over the investee to affect the amount of the investor's returns. [IFRS 10 para 7].
Subsidiary	An undertaking is a subsidiary of another undertaking if certain control criteria apply. [FRS 2 paras 14, 16].	Similar to old UK GAAP. A subsidiary is an entity that is controlled by a parent. [FRS 102 Glossary].	Similar to new UK GAAP and old UK GAAP. [IFRS 10 App A].
Consolidation			
Scope of consolidated financial statements	An undertaking is the parent undertaking of another undertaking (a subsidiary undertaking) where any of the following apply: • It holds a majority of voting rights. • It is a member and can appoint or remove directors holding a majority of voting rights. • It has the right to exercise dominant influence through provisions in the memorandum or articles or by control contract. • It has the power to exercise, or actually exercises, dominant influence or control over the undertaking, or it and the undertaking are managed on a unified basis. [FRS 2 para 14].	Similar to old UK GAAP. FRS 102 focuses on the concept of control in determining whether a parent/subsidiary relationship exists. Control is presumed to exist where a parent owns, directly or indirectly, more than 50% of an entity's voting power. Control also exists when a parent owns half or less of the voting power but has legal or contractual rights to control the majority of the entity's voting power or board of directors, or power to govern the financial and operating policies. Control can also be achieved by having convertible instruments that are currently exercisable. [FRS 102 paras 9.4-9.6].	Same as new UK GAAP; in addition, IFRS 10 provides extensive guidance to determine whether an investor controls an investee, including consideration of : • the purpose and design of the investee; • what the relevant activities are and who directs them; • the rights of the investor and any potential voting rights; • exposure to variable returns; • the ability to use power to affect returns; and • the investor's relationship with any other parties. [IFRS 10 App B].

	Old UK GAAP	New UK GAAP (FRS 102)	IFRS (IFRS 10 and IAS 27)
		Control can also exist where the parent has the power to exercise, or actually exercises, dominant influence or control over the undertaking, or it and the undertaking are managed on a unified basis. [FRS 102 para 9.6A].	
Requirement to prepare consolidated financial statements	A parent prepares consolidated financial statements, unless an exemption from this requirement is available (see below). The consolidated financial statements include the parent and all subsidiaries, except those required to be excluded (see below).	Under FRS 102, the consolidated financial statements include the parent and all subsidiaries, except those required to be excluded (see below). [FRS 102 para 9.2].	Under IFRS, parent entities prepare consolidated financial statements – unless an exemption is available (see below) – that include all subsidiaries. [IFRS 10 para 4].
Exemptions from consolidation	An exemption from consolidation is available: • for certain parent undertakings that are themselves subsidiary undertakings, and the immediate or ultimate parent produces consolidated financial statements that comply with EU Directives; • where all of a parent undertaking's subsidiaries are required or permitted to be excluded; and • where the group is small sized (as defined in company law).	As for old UK GAAP, the broader Companies Act exemption is maintained. The exemption for an intermediate parent is revised in the July 2015 amendments to FRS 102, to reflect changes in company law. In particular, if the company's parent owns 90% or more of the allotted shares, the exemption from consolidation is conditional on the remaining shareholders approving the exemption. [FRS 102 paras 9.1, 9.3].	IFRS provides an exemption for a parent entity that is itself a subsidiary. A parent need not present consolidated financial statements if: • the parent entity is itself wholly owned, or the other owners do not object to the parent not presenting consolidated financial statements; • the parent's securities are not publicly traded, and the parent is not in the process of issuing securities in public securities markets; and • the ultimate or intermediate parent produces IFRS financial statements. [IFRS 10 para 4]. This is narrower than the Companies Act exemption, which accepts equivalent GAAPs as well. *FRS 101 RDF (IFRS): Follow the current practice for EU IFRS reporters and first look to the Companies Act 2006 to establish whether consolidated accounts are needed. The Companies Act 2006 exemption exempts more subsidiaries than IFRS allows.*
Excluded subsidiaries	A subsidiary is excluded from consolidation if: • severe long-term restrictions substantially hinder the exercise of the parent undertaking's rights over the subsidiary's assets or management; or	FRS 102 is similar to old UK GAAP, except that: i. a subsidiary excluded from consolidation on the grounds of severe long-term restrictions is measured using an accounting policy selected by the parent in accordance with paragraph 26 of section 9 of FRS 102 (that is, cost, FVTOCI	Similar to new UK GAAP, except that IFRS 10 does not allow exclusion of a subsidiary from the consolidation because the parent is a venture capital or similar organisation. IFRS 10 does not specifically mention the exclusion from

	Old UK GAAP	New UK GAAP (FRS 102)	IFRS (IFRS 10 and IAS 27)
	• the subsidiary is held exclusively with a view to subsequent resale and it has not previously been consolidated. [FRS 2 paras 21, 23, 25, 27, 29].	or FVTPL), except where there is significant influence, in which case the equity method set out in section 14 of FRS 102 is used, and ii. the definition of 'held exclusively with a view to subsequent resale' is expanded to include entities held as part of an investment portfolio. These entities are measured at fair value with changes to profit or loss. [FRS 102 paras 9.9, 9.9A, 9.9B, 9.26]. In line with old UK GAAP, FRS 102 does not allow exclusion of a subsidiary from the consolidation for dissimilar activities, or because the information necessary for the preparation of consolidated financial statements cannot be obtained without disproportionate expense or undue delay. [FRS 102 paras 9.8, 9.8A].	consolidation due to the restriction in the transfer of funds to the parent company. A subsidiary that is acquired, held exclusively with a view to disposal and meets the definition of an asset held for sale, is not excluded from consolidation. However, it is measured and accounted for under IFRS 5, initially at fair value less costs to sell. Under IFRS 10, if an entity qualifies as an investment entity, it should only consolidate subsidiaries that provide services related to its investment activities. All other subsidiaries should not be consolidated, nor should IFRS 3 be applied, where it obtains control of these entities. Instead, an investment entity measures an investment in these subsidiaries at fair value through profit or loss in accordance with IFRS 9. [IFRS 10 paras 31-32].
Quasi-subsidiaries/special purpose entities (SPEs)	Where another entity (a 'vehicle') gives rise to benefits for the reporting entity that are, in substance, no different from those that would arise if the vehicle were a subsidiary, it is consolidated if there is control. In determining whether the reporting entity controls a vehicle, management should take into account who, in practice, directs the financial and operating policies of the vehicle. [FRS 2 para 64; FRS 5 paras 7, 32-38].	Similar to old UK GAAP. An SPE is an entity created to accomplish a narrow, well-defined objective. An entity consolidates an SPE where the substance of the relationship between the entity and the SPE indicates that the SPE is controlled by the entity. The following circumstances may indicate that an entity controls an SPE (this is not an exhaustive list): • the activities of the SPE are being conducted on behalf of the entity according to its specific business needs; • the entity has the ultimate decision-making powers over the activities of the SPE, even if the day-to-day decisions have been delegated; • the entity has rights to obtain the majority of the benefits of the SPE, and therefore may be exposed to risks incidental to the activities of the SPE; and • the entity retains the majority of the residual or ownership risks related to the SPE or its assets. [FRS 102 para 9.11].	IFRS 10 (and IFRS 12) refer to 'structured entities' instead of SPEs. [IFRS 12 App A]. Most entities that are SPEs will also be structured entities under IFRS 10 and IFRS 12. However, given that the guidance has changed, some SPEs may not be structured entities under the requirements of the new standards, and vice versa. The control assessment framework in IFRS 10 is equally applicable to all types of entities, including structured entities. The following matters need to be considered when assessing who has the power to direct a structured entity's relevant activities under IFRS 10 and IFRS 12: • Involvement in (and decisions made at) the structured entity's inception as part of its design (purpose and design). • Whether voting or similar rights are dominant, such that they convey substantive decision

	Old UK GAAP	New UK GAAP (FRS 102)	IFRS (IFRS 10 and IAS 27)
			making powers, or whether substantive powers have been prescribed through contractual terms (for example, an 'autopilot' arrangement). • Rights to direct the structured entity's relevant activities that are only activated when certain events occur. • Commitments to ensure that the structured entity operates in the way designed. • *De facto* agent analysis. • Whether an investor should treat a portion of an investee as a deemed separate entity ('silo' analysis). [IFRS 10 App B paras B5-B8, B51-B54, B73-B77; IFRS 12 App B paras B22-B24].
Disposal of subsidiaries	The consolidated profit and loss account should include the trading results of the undertaking up to the date of its ceasing to be a subsidiary. Any gain or loss arising on disposal is included in the profit and loss account. The profit or loss on disposal of a subsidiary is the difference at the date of disposal between the following amounts: • the carrying amount attributable to the group's interest in the subsidiary's net assets (including goodwill) after the disposal or partial disposal, together with any proceeds received ; and • the group's interests in the subsidiary's net assets (including goodwill) before the disposal. [FRS 2 paras 46-48]. A partial disposal arises where a subsidiary: • remains a subsidiary, but with a reduced interest; • becomes an associate or joint venture; or • becomes an investment.	Similar to old UK GAAP. In addition, the gain or loss arising on the disposal should include those amounts that have been recognised in other comprehensive income in relation to that subsidiary, where those amounts are required to be reclassified to profit or loss on disposal, in accordance with other sections of FRS 102. [FRS 102 paras 9.18A-9.18B].	Similar to new UK GAAP. [IFRS 10 App B para B97-B99]. However, IFRS 10 also requires a parent entity to: • Remeasure any retained interest at fair value (in a partial disposal) in the event of loss of control. [IFRS 10 App B para 98]. • Separately disclose both the total gain or loss on the loss of control of the subsidiary, and the portion of the gain or loss related to the retained non-controlling investment. [IFRS 12 para 19].

	Old UK GAAP	New UK GAAP (FRS 102)	IFRS (IFRS 10 and IAS 27)
	If the group has adopted FRS 23, the cumulative exchange differences previously taken to reserves on the translation of the net investment in that subsidiary should also be included in the gain or loss on disposal. [FRS 23 para 48].	The cumulative amount of any exchange differences that relate to a foreign subsidiary recognised in equity is not recognised in profit or loss as part of the gain or loss on disposal of the subsidiary, and should be transferred directly to retained earnings. [FRS 102 para 9.18A].	Same as old UK GAAP (FRS 23). [IAS 21 para 48].
Minority interest/ presentation of non-controlling interest (NCI)	The aggregate capital and reserves attributable to the minority are shown separately from capital and reserves in the consolidated balance sheet. The aggregate profit or loss attributable to the minority is shown separately in the consolidated profit and loss account as a deduction against profits. [FRS 2 paras 35-36].	Similar to old UK GAAP. However, profit or loss and each component of other comprehensive income are attributed to the non-controlling interest (rather than being shown as a deduction) and the parent's owners. [FRS 102 paras 4.2, 9.13, 9.20-9.22].	Same as new UK GAAP. [IAS 1 paras 27-28, 54(q), 83; IFRS 10 paras 22-24].
Losses attributable to minority interest/NCI	Profits or losses are apportioned between the controlling and minority interests. Where losses attributable to the minority interest result in its interest being net liabilities, the group should make a provision to the extent that it has any commercial or legal obligation to provide finance that may not be recoverable in respect of the accumulated losses attributable to the minority interest. [FRS 2 para 37; SI 2008/410 6 Sch 17(3)]. In our view, as losses are incurred by a subsidiary, the minority's share of these losses will: • first, be set against the minority's share of the subsidiary's reserves; • secondly, be set against the minority's share of the subsidiary's capital ; and • finally, be recognised as a debit balance in the consolidated balance sheet to the extent that the group does not have a commercial or legal obligation in respect of the losses attributable to the minority interests. The above process should be reversed where profits attributable to the minority start to make good the losses incurred previously.	Profits or losses are allocated to parent's owners and the non-controlling interest, even if this results in the NCI having a deficit balance. [FRS 102 para 9.22]. There is no additional guidance relating to deficit NCI balances. However, we would expect a similar approach as that for old UK GAAP to apply for dealing with subsequent profits.	Losses are attributed to owners of the parent and NCI, even if this results in the NCI having a deficit balance. [IFRS 10 App B paras 94-96]. Where a loss-making subsidiary subsequently reports profits, those profits are allocated in proportion to the respective interests of the controlling and non-controlling interest.

	Old UK GAAP	New UK GAAP (FRS 102)	IFRS (IFRS 10 and IAS 27)
Transactions with minority interest/NCI	Where an entity buys a minority interest and keeps control, the assets and liabilities of the subsidiary are revalued to fair value and with a consequential adjustment to goodwill. [FRS 2 para 51]. Where an entity sells a minority interest but keeps control, any gain or loss on disposal is included in profit or loss. [FRS 2 para 52].	Transactions with NCI where the entity retains control are recognised in equity in the same way as treasury share transactions. Goodwill is not adjusted. [FRS 102 para 22.19].	Same as new UK GAAP. [IFRS 10 paras 23-24, App B paras B94-B96].
Written put options over NCI	A liability is recognised for management's best estimate of the present value of the put option's redemption amount. [FRS 25 para 23].	There are two possible methods of accounting for such an instrument with the appropriate treatment depending on the substance of the transaction: • Put options written at the same time as a business combination are in substance a puttable instrument for which a liability at the present value of the redemption amount is recognised in the consolidated financial statements. • A written put over an entity's own shares which is not entered into in connection with a business combination should be accounted for consistently with other derivatives on own shares (that is, as an equity instrument if 'fixed for fixed' is met or as a (derivative) financial instrument at fair value through P&L if 'fixed for fixed' is not met). [FRS 102 para 22.5(d)].	An entity that has an obligation to purchase its own equity instruments for cash or another financial asset records a liability at the present value of the redemption amount. This is the case even if the contract is an equity instrument itself. [IAS 32 para 23].
Accounting policies	Uniform accounting policies should be used for determining the amounts to be included in the consolidated financial statements, except in exceptional cases; such a departure should be explained in the financial statements. [FRS 2 paras 40-41].	Similar to old UK GAAP. Consolidated financial statements are prepared by using uniform accounting policies for like transactions, and events in similar circumstances, for all of the entities in a group. [FRS 102 para 9.17].	Same as new UK GAAP. [IFRS 10 para 19].
Intra-group balances and transactions	Intra-group transactions, balances and unrealised profits are eliminated in full. [FRS 2 para 39].	Same as old UK GAAP. [FRS 102 para 9.15].	Same as new UK GAAP and old UK GAAP. [IFRS 10 App B para B86(c)].
Reporting periods	The financial statements of all subsidiary undertakings to be used in preparing the consolidated financial statements are, wherever practicable, prepared to the same financial year	Similar to old UK GAAP. The consolidated financial statements of the parent and its subsidiaries are usually drawn up at the same	Similar to new UK GAAP, except that IFRS allows the use of a subsidiary's financial year ending up to three months before or after the

	Old UK GAAP	**New UK GAAP (FRS 102)**	**IFRS (IFRS 10 and IAS 27)**
	end and for the same accounting period as those of the parent undertaking.	reporting date, unless it is impracticable to do so. [FRS 102 para 9.16].	parent's year end. [IFRS 10 App B paras B92-B93].
	Where the financial year of a subsidiary undertaking differs from that of the parent undertaking, interim financial statements are prepared to the same date as those of the parent for use in the preparation of the consolidated financial statements. If it is not practicable to draw up interim financial statements at the same date, the last financial year of the subsidiary may be used if this is three months or less before the parent's year end, adjusted if necessary for significant transactions that occur in the gap period . [Companies Act 2006; SI 2008/409; SI 2008/410 6 Sch 2(2); FRS 2 paras 42-43].	As for old UK GAAP, the guidance in FRS 102 provides that, where the reporting date of a subsidiary differs from its parent, the Companies Act requirements should be followed. [FRS 102 para 9.16].	
Separate financial statements			
Separate financial statements	In the investor's separate financial statements, its interests in associates are treated as fixed asset investments. They are shown either at cost less any amounts written off, or at valuation. Changes in valuation are recognised in the statement of total recognised gains and losses. [FRS 9 paras 20, 26].	Where separate financial statements of a parent are prepared, the entity chooses to account for its investments in subsidiaries, jointly controlled entities and associates, either: • at cost less impairment; • at fair value through profit or loss; or • at fair value through other comprehensive income. The same accounting policies do not have to be applied to all three categories (subsidiaries, jointly controlled entities and associates). [FRS 102 para 9.26].	Where separate financial statements of a parent are prepared, the entity accounts for investments in subsidiaries, jointly controlled entities and associates either: • at cost; or • in accordance with IFRS 9. Also, investments held for sale are addressed in IFRS 5. The measurement of investments accounted for at fair value under IFRS 9 is not changed where they are classified as held for sale under IFRS 5. [IAS 27 para 10].

Business combinations

Under old UK GAAP, business combinations were normally accounted for by acquisition accounting. Merger accounting was used if certain criteria were met, but this was rare in practice outside group reconstructions. IFRS requires the use of the purchase method of accounting for business combination transactions that are not common control transactions. New UK GAAP (FRS 102) generally requires use of the purchase method, but it allows merger accounting to be applied to group reconstructions (subject to new conditions for its use in company law).

The requirements in FRS 102 are based on IFRS 3, 'Business combinations', before it was revised in 2008. There are, therefore, some differences between the requirements for business combinations in FRS 102 and those in the current version of IFRS 3. The old UK GAAP requirements within FRS 6 and FRS 7 are closer to FRS 102 than IFRS.

	Old UK GAAP	New UK GAAP (FRS 102)	IFRS
Scope of the standard	FRS 6 and FRS 7 apply to all business combinations. They apply where an entity becomes a subsidiary of a parent that prepares consolidated financial statements, and where a separate company combines with a business other than a subsidiary undertaking. Group reconstructions are within the scope of the accounting requirements of FRS 6 and FRS 7. [FRS 6 para 4; FRS 7 para 4].	Combinations involving the formation of a joint venture are excluded from the scope. [FRS 102 para 19.2]. Group reconstructions are within the scope . [FRS 102 para 19.27]. In addition, public benefit entities have to consider the requirements of section 34 of FRS 102 in accounting for public benefit entity combinations. [FRS 102 para PBE19.2A]. Subsidiaries held as part of an investment portfolio are dealt with by section 9 of FRS 102 (and measured at fair value through profit or loss).	The formation of any type of joint arrangement is excluded from IFRS 3's scope. [IFRS 3 para 2]. Combinations involving entities or businesses under common control are excluded from IFRS 3's scope . Further guidance on common control is provided. [IFRS 3 paras 2, B1-B4]. IFRS 3's scope also excludes the acquisition by an investment entity (as defined in IFRS 10) of an investment in a subsidiary that is required to be measured at fair value through profit or loss. [IFRS 3 para 2A].
Definitions			
Business	'Business' is not a defined term in old UK GAAP.	A business is an integrated set of activities and assets conducted and managed for the purpose of providing either a return to investors or lower costs or other economic benefits directly and proportionately to policyholders or participants. [FRS 102 Glossary].	Similar to new UK GAAP, except that, in order to qualify as a business, the integrated set of activities and assets need only be capable of being conducted and managed . [IFRS 3 App A].
Business combination	The bringing together of separate entities into one economic entity as a result of one entity uniting with, or obtaining control over the net assets and operations of, another. [FRS 6 para 2].	The bringing together of separate entities or businesses into one reporting entity. [FRS 102 para 19.3].	A transaction or other event in which an acquirer obtains control of one or more businesses. [IFRS 3 App A].
Acquisition date	This is the date on which control of the acquired entity passes to the acquirer. [FRS 7 para 2].	Same as old UK GAAP. [FRS 102 para 19.3].	Same as new UK GAAP and old UK GAAP. [IFRS 3 para 8].

	Old UK GAAP	New UK GAAP (FRS 102)	IFRS
Accounting			
Purchase accounting	FRS 6 sets out specified criteria for determining whether a business combination is a merger. If the combination does not meet these criteria, it is an acquisition. [FRS 6 para 20]. Under acquisition accounting, the identifiable assets and liabilities of the acquired entities are included in the acquirer's consolidated balance sheet at their fair value at the date of acquisition. The difference between the fair value of the net identifiable assets acquired and the fair value of the purchase consideration is goodwill. [FRS 6 para 20].	All business combinations are accounted for using the purchase method, except for: • group reconstructions, which may be accounted for using merger accounting ; and • public benefit entity combinations that are in substance a gift or that are a merger accounted for under section 34 of FRS 102. [FRS 102 para 19.6]. The steps involved in applying the purchase method are: • identify the acquirer; • measure the cost of the business combination; and • allocate the cost of the business combination to the identifiable assets acquired, and liabilities and contingent liabilities assumed, at the acquisition date. [FRS 102 para 19.7].	IFRS 3 does not have a cost allocation model. The fair value of acquired assets and liabilities (with some exceptions) is compared to the fair value of the consideration to determine goodwill. [IFRS 3 para 32].
Identifying the acquirer	FRS 6 does not require an acquirer to be identified for all business combinations. If no party to the combination obtains control over any other, or is otherwise seen to be dominant, merger accounting is used (but this is rare in practice). [FRS 6 para 6].	An acquirer is identified for all business combinations accounted for under the purchase method. The acquirer is the combining entity that obtains control of the other combining entities or businesses. Examples of indicators to identify the acquirer include: • the larger of the relative fair value of the combining entities; • the giving up of cash or other assets in a business combination where they were exchanged for voting ordinary equity instruments; and • the power of management of a combining entity to dominate the management of the combined entity. [FRS 102 paras 19.8 –19.10].	Similar to new UK GAAP. In addition, IFRS 3 includes more extensive guidance on indicators to identify the acquirer. [IFRS 3 paras 6 –7, App B, paras B13-B18].

	Old UK GAAP	**New UK GAAP (FRS 102)**	**IFRS**
Cost of acquisition	The cost of an acquisition is the amount of cash paid and the fair value of other purchase consideration given by the acquirer, together with the expenses of the acquisition. Such expenses should be incremental and directly attributable to the acquisition. [FRS 7 paras 26, 85].	Similar to old UK GAAP. The cost of a business combination includes the fair value of assets given, liabilities incurred or assumed, and equity instruments issued by the acquirer in exchange for the control of the acquiree, plus any directly attributable costs. [FRS 102 para 19.11].	The fair value of consideration transferred excludes the transaction costs (which are expensed) and requires re-measurement of any previously held interest at fair value as part of the consideration. [IFRS 3 paras 37, 53]. Consideration excludes amounts paid to settle pre-existing relationships and other separate arrangements that are not part of the exchange for the acquiree. [IFRS 3 para 51].
Share-based consideration	Shares issued as consideration are recorded at their fair value on the date of acquisition. UK GAAP includes guidance on determining the fair value of shares issued as consideration. [FRS 7 paras 26, 76, 78].	Same as old UK GAAP. [FRS 102 para 19.11].	Similar to new UK GAAP and old UK GAAP for measurement of equity instruments given as part of the consideration. IFRS includes further guidance where the acquirer's share-based payments awards are exchanged for awards held by the acquiree's employees. [IFRS 3 para 37].
Adjustments to the cost of a business combination contingent on future events (contingent consideration)	Where the amount of purchase consideration is contingent on one or more future events, the cost of acquisition should include a reasonable estimate of the fair value of amounts expected to be payable in the future.	Similar to old UK GAAP, but a probability test is applied at the date of acquisition. Contingent consideration is included as part of the cost at the date of the acquisition if it is probable (that is, more likely than not) that the amount will be paid and can be measured reliably.	Contingent consideration is recognised initially at fair value as either a financial liability or equity, regardless of the probability of payment. The probability of payment is included in the fair value, which is deemed to be reliably measurable.
	The cost of acquisition is adjusted when revised estimates of the amount expected to be paid are made. [FRS 7 paras 27, 81].	Changes (including becoming probable) to contingent consideration adjust the cost of the combination. [FRS 102 paras 19.12-19.13].	Financial liabilities arising from contingent consideration arrangements are remeasured to fair value at each reporting date, with the changes recognised in profit or loss. Equity-classified contingent consideration is not remeasured at each reporting date; its settlement is accounted for within equity. Any financial asset (for example, contingently returnable consideration) is adjusted via profit or loss or (for acquisitions prior to 1 July 2014) other comprehensive income, as appropriate. [IFRS 3 paras 39, 58]. *FRS 101 RDF (IFRS): IFRS 3 was amended by FRS 101 to move from a fair value model for contingent consideration to recognition at best estimate if probable, with adjustments being made against goodwill. [FRS 101 para AG1(d),(e)]. This amendment to IFRS has been removed in the*

	Old UK GAAP	New UK GAAP (FRS 102)	IFRS
			July 2015 amendments to FRS 101 to reflect changes to the fair value accounting rules in company law; so the IFRS treatment will apply going forward, subject to amended transitional rules in FRS 101.
Allocating the cost of a business	The identifiable assets and liabilities to be recognised are those of the acquired entity that existed at the date of acquisition. The recognised assets and liabilities are measured at fair values that reflect the conditions at the date of the acquisition. [FRS 7 paras 5-6].	Similar to old UK GAAP. The acquirer recognises separately the acquiree's identifiable assets, liabilities and contingent liabilities that existed at the date of acquisition. These assets and liabilities are recognised at fair value at the date of acquisition, except for deferred tax, employee benefit arrangements and share-based payment where the relevant section of FRS 102 applies. [FRS 102 paras 19.14, 19.15A-19.15C].	Similar to new UK GAAP, in that assets and liabilities are generally recognised at fair value at the acquisition date; however, exceptions to fair value measurement apply, including for reacquired rights (based on contractual terms), replacement of share-based payment awards (in accordance with IFRS 2), income tax (IAS 12), employee benefits (IAS 19), indemnification assets and assets held for sale. [IFRS 3 paras 18, 24-31]. IFRS has more detailed fair value measurement guidance (in IFRS 13) than FRS 102.
Restructuring provision	Provisions for future reorganisations, operating losses and integration costs expected to be incurred as a result of the acquisition, whether they related to the acquired entity or the acquirer, do not affect fair values at the date of acquisition; they are therefore treated as post-acquisition expenses. [FRS 7 para 7(c)]. In the case of restructuring decisions made by the acquired entity before the date of acquisition, the principles for recognising consequential provisions on acquisition are set out in paragraph 18 of FRS 3. [FRS 7 para 38].	Same as old UK GAAP. [FRS 102 para 19.18].	Similar to new UK GAAP and old UK GAAP; however, there is further guidance that, where a restructuring plan is conditional on the completion of the business combination, it is not recognised in the accounting for the acquisition. These expenses are recognised post-acquisition. [IFRS 3 para 11].
Employee benefits	Where an acquired entity sponsors a defined benefit pension scheme, the allocation of fair values includes an asset or liability in respect of any surplus or deficit in the fund. [FRS 7 paras 19 -20, 70-73].	An asset or liability related to the acquiree's employee benefit arrangements is recognised and measured in accordance with section 28 of FRS 102. [FRS 102 para 19.15B].	An asset or liability related to the acquiree's employee benefit arrangements is recognised in accordance with IAS 19. [IFRS 3 para 26].
Contingent liabilities	Contingent assets and liabilities are measured at fair values, where these can be determined. [FRS 7 para 15].	Acquired contingent liabilities are recognised separately at the acquisition date as a part of allocation of the cost, provided their fair values can be measured reliably. [FRS 102 paras 19.20-19.21].	Same as new UK GAAP. [IFRS 3 paras 23, 56, BC276].

	Old UK GAAP	New UK GAAP (FRS 102)	IFRS
		However, contingent assets do not meet the definition of 'assets' in the framework, so they are not recognised in a business combination. If an asset exists at the date of acquisition, being an unconditional right, it is not a contingent asset and it is recognised at fair value. [FRS 102 paras 19.15, 21.13].	
Initial accounting determined provisionally	Any necessary adjustments to provisional fair values (together with a corresponding adjustment to goodwill) are incorporated in the financial statements for the first full financial year following the acquisition. [FRS 7 paras 23-25].	The acquirer retrospectively adjusts provisional values recognised within 12 months of the acquisition date, with a corresponding adjustment to goodwill. [FRS 102 para 19.19].	Same as new UK GAAP. [IFRS 3 para 62].
Minority interest/non-controlling interests	Minority interest is defined as the interest in a subsidiary undertaking included in the consolidation that is attributable to the shares held by or on behalf of persons other than the parent undertaking. [FRS 2 para 13]. The partial goodwill method is applied – that is, goodwill arising on acquisition is only recognised with respect to the part of the subsidiary undertaking that is attributable to the interest held by the parent and its other subsidiary undertakings. No goodwill is attributed to the minority interest. [FRS 2 para 38].	The non-controlling interest is measured at the date of the combination at its share in the net amount of the identifiable assets, liabilities and contingent liabilities recognised and measured in accordance with section 19 of FRS 102. [FRS 102 para 9.13(d)].	For each business combination, the acquirer measures any non-controlling interest in the acquirer either at fair value (full goodwill method) or at the non-controlling interest's proportionate share of the acquiree's identifiable net assets (partial goodwill method). [IFRS 3 para 19].
Acquiring a subsidiary undertakings in stages	Company law requires the identifiable assets and liabilities of a subsidiary undertaking to be included in the consolidation at fair value at the date of its acquisition. Paragraph 26 of FRS 7 states that, where a subsidiary is acquired in stages, the cost of acquisition is the total of the costs of the interests acquired, determined at the date of each transaction. However, in some circumstances, it may be appropriate to use a true and fair override of company law in order to use fair values at the dates of earlier purchases. [FRS 2 paras 50, 89].	Where a group acquires control of a subsidiary in stages, it accounts for it as follows: • the business combination's cost is the aggregate of the fair values of the assets given, liabilities assumed and equity instruments issued by the acquirer at the date of each transaction in the series; and • the combination's cost is allocated by recognising the acquired assets, liabilities and contingent liabilities at their fair values at the acquisition date (that is, when control is obtained), unless exceptions apply). [FRS 102 paras 9.19B, 19.11A, 19.14].	The acquirer re measures its previously held equity interest in the acquiree at its fair value at the acquisition date, and recognises the resulting gain or loss, if any, in profit or loss. [IFRS 3 para 42].

	Old UK GAAP	New UK GAAP (FRS 102)	IFRS
Goodwill			
Goodwill	Goodwill is the difference between the cost of an acquisition and the aggregate of the fair values of that entity's identifiable assets and liabilities. Positive purchased goodwill is capitalised and classified as an intangible asset on the balance sheet.	Similar to old UK GAAP. Goodwill (that is, the excess of the cost of the business combination over the acquirer's interest in the net fair value of the identifiable assets, liabilities and contingent liabilities) is recognised as an intangible asset at the acquisition date. [FRS 102 para 19.22].	Goodwill is the difference between the sum of the consideration transferred, plus the amount of any non-controlling interest, plus the fair value of any previously held interest and the net fair value of the identifiable assets, liabilities and contingent liabilities.
	After initial recognition, goodwill is amortised on a systematic basis over its useful life – this is presumed to be 20 years if the entity is unable to make a reliable estimate of the useful life. Where goodwill is regarded as having an indefinite useful economic life, it is not amortised. Goodwill amortised over more than 20 years (or not amortised) is reviewed for impairment at the end of each period using FRS 11. [FRS 10 paras 2, 15, 17, 19, 37].	After initial recognition, goodwill is measured at cost less accumulated amortisation and any accumulated impairment losses. Goodwill is amortised over its useful life. In exceptional cases, if a reliable estimate is not possible, the life should not exceed five years (increased to 10 years under the July 2015 amendments to FRS 102). [FRS 102 para 19.23]. It is expected that entities transitioning from old UK GAAP to FRS 102 will maintain their existing life for goodwill.	Amortisation of goodwill is not permitted. Goodwill is subject to an impairment test annually and where there is an indicator of impairment. *FRS 101 RDF (IFRS): Non-amortisation of goodwill is usually a departure from the Companies Act 2006 for the overriding purpose of giving a true and fair view. Disclosure of the departure and its effect are required. [FRS 101 paras AG1(f), A2.8].* The option provided by IFRS to measure the non-controlling interest, using either fair value method or proportionate share method on each transaction, may result in different goodwill amounts. This option is on a transaction-by-transaction basis. [IFRS 3 para 32; IAS 36 paras 9-10].
Negative goodwill	Negative goodwill is shown as a separate (negative) item on the asset side of the balance sheet (once management has reassessed the identification and measurement of other assets and liabilities arising on acquisition) and is subsequently recognised as income: • in the periods in which the non-monetary assets acquired are recovered through depreciation or sale (but only to the extent of those assets); or • otherwise, in the periods expected to be benefited. [FRS 10 paras 48-50].	Same as old UK GAAP. [FRS 102 para 19.24].	IFRS 3 uses the term 'gain on bargain purchase' instead of 'negative goodwill'. It is recognised in profit or loss immediately after management has reassessed the identification and measurement of other assets and liabilities arising on acquisition and the cost of the business combination. [IFRS 3 paras 34, 36]. *FRS 101 RDF (IFRS): Negative goodwill is recognised up to the fair value of non-monetary assets acquired in profit or loss in the periods in which the non-monetary assets are recovered. Any negative goodwill exceeding the fair value of non-monetary assets acquired is recognised in profit or*

	Old UK GAAP	New UK GAAP (FRS 102)	IFRS
			loss in the periods expected to be benefited. [FRS 101 para AG1(c)].
Reverse acquisition accounting	UK company law and accounting standards (old UK GAAP) do not envisage reverse acquisition accounting, but a true and fair override of these may be required in certain circumstances.	FRS 102 does not refer to a reverse acquisition, but the requirement to identify the acquirer is similar in principle to IFRS. However, UK company law does not envisage reverse acquisition accounting so this would involve a true and fair override.	A reverse acquisition arises in a business combination where the 'acquired entity' (or its owners) controls the combined entity and is identified as the acquirer under IFRS 3. Guidance on reverse acquisition accounting is provided in Appendix B to IFRS 3.
Merger accounting	Merger accounting for a business combination is required if it is not prohibited by company legislation and the combination meets the criteria set out in paragraphs 6-11 of FRS 6. [FRS 6 para 5]. Under merger accounting, the carrying values of the combining parties' assets and liabilities are not adjusted to fair value on consolidation, although appropriate adjustments should be made to achieve uniformity of accounting policies. [FRS 6 paras 16-18]. Merger expenses are charged to the profit and loss account at the effective date of the merger as non-operating restructuring expenses. [FRS 6 para 19].	Merger accounting may only be applied to group reconstructions, and, where permitted by the relevant statutory framework, to public benefit entity combinations that meet the definition of a merger. [FRS 102 paras 19.6, PBE34.80]. The merger accounting method is the same as old UK GAAP. [FRS 102 paras 19.29-19.31]. Merger expenses are charged to the income account at the effective date of the combination as part of profit or loss of the combined entity. [FRS 102 para 19.32].	Merger accounting (or 'uniting of interests') is not permitted by IFRS 3 for business combinations within its scope.
Accounting for group reconstructions/common control transactions	Under FRS 6, merger accounting can also be used to account for certain forms of group reconstruction. A group reconstruction may be accounted for by using merger accounting (even if it does not meet the definition of a merger), provided: • the ultimate shareholders remain the same, and the rights of each such shareholder, relative to the others, are unchanged; • no minority's interest in the net assets of the group is altered by the transfer; and • the use of merger accounting is not prohibited by company legislation. [FRS 6 para 13].	The accounting for group reconstructions under FRS 102 is the same as in old UK GAAP*. [FRS 102 para 19.27]. *However, the conditions in company law for use of merger accounting have changed. These are now similar to the conditions for common control transactions in IFRS 3, and differ from the conditions in section 19 of FRS 102 for group reconstructions. The legal appendix to FRS 102 has been updated in the July 2015 amendments to refer to use of the true and fair override for some group reconstructions if an entity considers that this is necessary in order to apply merger accounting in circumstances other than those set out in the company law. [FRS 102 para A4.30].	There is no guidance in IFRS in relation to accounting for business combinations between entities under common control. Management therefore makes an accounting policy election in relation to the most appropriate accounting for its circumstances. In practice, such transactions are generally accounted for using merger accounting. [IFRS 3 paras 2, B1-B4].

Discontinued operations and assets held for sale

Old UK GAAP and new UK GAAP (FRS 102) do not have 'held for sale' classification for non-financial assets or groups of assets and liabilities, unlike IFRS 5, 'Non-current assets held for sale and discontinued operations'. Instead, a decision to sell an asset is considered an impairment indicator, which triggers an impairment review. Discontinued operations are taken into account, but not in a separate section.

	Old UK GAAP	New UK GAAP (FRS 102)	IFRS
Discontinued operations – definition	There is no UK equivalent standard in relation to non-current assets or disposal groups held for sale. Where an operation is terminated, it qualifies as discontinued in a period if the termination takes place in the period or before the earlier of three months after commencement of the subsequent accounting period and the date on which the financial statements are approved. The activities must have ceased permanently in this period. [FRS 3 para 4]. Subsidiaries acquired exclusively with a view to resale are reasonably expected to be disposed of within approximately one year of the date of acquisition. They are excluded from consolidation and are accounted for as current assets at the lower of cost and net realisable value. [FRS 2 paras 11, 25].	A discontinued operation is a component of an entity that has been disposed of. It represents a separate major line of business or geographical area of operations, or was part of a single coordinated plan to dispose of a major line of business or geographical area of operations. It could also be a subsidiary acquired exclusively for resale. [FRS 102 Glossary].	Similar to new UK GAAP, but also refers to a component of an entity that is held for sale (see below). [IFRS 5 para 32].
Presentation	The following is disclosed for discontinued operations: • Continuing and discontinued operations are disclosed separately, in the profit and loss account; the minimum that is disclosed in respect of discontinued operations is turnover and operating profit. • Analysis of other line items between turnover and operating profit may be given in the profit and loss account or in the notes. Tax and interest may be allocated, but the basis should be stated. [FRS 3 para 14]. Material effects of disposals (and acquisitions) on amounts reported under each of the standard cash flow statement headings are given. Disclosure of	An analysis between continuing operations and discontinued operations is disclosed for each of the line items on the face of the statement of comprehensive income (and, if presented separately, the income statement). The income statement should also present an amount comprising the total of: a. the discontinued operation's post-tax profit or loss; and b. the post-tax gain or loss attributable to the impairment or on the disposal of a discontinued operation. The line-by-line analysis should be presented in a columnar format for continuing and discontinued operations; a total column should also be	Discontinued operations are presented separately in the statement of comprehensive income and the statement of cash flows. There are additional disclosure requirements in relation to discontinued operations. [IFRS 5 para 33]. *FRS 101 RDF (IFRS): The analysis of discontinued operations is shown in the statement of comprehensive income in a columnar format; it cannot be presented in the notes. [FRS 101 para AG1(g)].*

	Old UK GAAP	New UK GAAP (FRS 102)	IFRS
	cash flows from discontinued operations is encouraged. [FRS 1 paras 45, 56].	presented to comply with the Act's requirements for statutory totals. [FRS 102 paras 5.7D, 5.7E, App].	
Non-current assets held for sale	There is no old UK standard in relation to non-current assets or disposal groups held for sale. However, a non-current asset to be disposed of forms an income-generating unit of its own and is written down to its recoverable amount (higher of net realisable value and value in use). [FRS 11 paras 14, 31].	Not covered. The decision to sell an asset, or plans to discontinue the operation to which an asset belongs, are considered an impairment indicator. [FRS 102 para 27.9(f)].	A non-current asset (or disposal group) is classified as 'held for sale' if its carrying amount is recovered principally through a sale transaction rather than through continuing use. This is the case where the asset (or disposal group) is available for immediate sale in its present condition, its sale is highly probable and the sale is expected to be completed within one year from the date of classification. Assets (or disposal groups) classified for sale are: • carried at the lower of the carrying amount and fair value less costs to sell; • not depreciated or amortised; and • presented separately in the statement of financial position. [IFRS 5 paras 1, 6-7, 15, 38].

Investments in associates

	Old UK GAAP	New UK GAAP (FRS 102)	IFRS
Definition	An associate is an entity (other than a subsidiary) in which the investor has a participating interest and exercises significant influence. [FRS 9 para 4].	Similar to old UK GAAP. An associate is an entity over which the investor has significant influence, but that is neither a subsidiary nor a joint venture of the investor. [FRS 102 para 14.2].	Same as new UK GAAP. [IAS 28 para 3].
Significant influence	Exercise of significant influence is where the investor is actively involved and is influential in policy decisions, including strategic issues. The decisive feature is the actual relationship between investor and investee. Company law provides that an entity holding 20% or more of the voting rights in another entity is presumed to exercise significant influence over that entity unless the contrary is shown. [FRS 9 para 4].	Similar to old UK GAAP. Significant influence is the power to participate in the financial and operating policy decisions of the associate but is not control or joint control over those policies. It is presumed to exist where the investor holds at least 20% of the investee's voting power; it is presumed not to exist where less than 20% is held. These presumptions may be rebutted if there is clear evidence to the contrary. The main difference from old UK GAAP is that significant influence does not have to be exercised. [FRS 102 para 14.3].	Similar to old UK GAAP and new UK GAAP; in addition, IFRS gives the following indicators of significant influence to be considered where the investor holds less than 20% of the voting power of the investee: • representation on the board of directors or equivalent body; • participation in policy-making processes; • material transactions between the investor and the investee;

	Old UK GAAP	New UK GAAP (FRS 102)	IFRS
			• interchange of managerial personnel; and • provision of essential technical information. The existence and effect of potential voting rights that are currently exercisable or convertible are considered when assessing whether an entity has significant influence. [IAS 28 paras 6-8].
Accounting for associates	An investment in an associate is accounted for in consolidated financial statements using the equity method. [FRS 9 para 26]. However, certain investment funds are permitted to include all investments in their investment portfolio (including those over which they have significant influence) either at cost or at market value. [FRS 9 para 49].	In its consolidated financial statements, an investor accounts for an associate by using the equity method of accounting. If the associate is held as part of an investment portfolio, it is measured at fair value with changes recognised in profit or loss. [FRS 102 paras 14.4A-14.4B].	Similar to old UK GAAP and new UK GAAP. Investments in associates are accounted for using the equity method. Some exceptions are in place – for example, where the investment is classified as held for sale, or for investments in associates held by venture capital organisations, mutual funds, unit trusts and similar entities (see below). [IAS 28 para 17].
Equity method	FRS 9 defines the equity method as a method of accounting that brings an investment into its investor's financial statements initially at its cost (which typically includes transaction costs), identifying any goodwill arising.	Similar to old UK GAAP. An associate is initially recognised at the transaction price (including transaction costs). The investor, on acquisition of the investment, accounts for the difference between the cost of the acquisition and its share of fair value of the net identifiable assets as goodwill, which is included in the carrying amount of the investment (as part of the transaction price). [FRS 102 para 14.8].	Similar to old UK GAAP and new UK GAAP. Initial recognition of an investment in an associate is at cost. Cost usually includes transaction costs under IFRS, and therefore it is appropriate to include such costs in the initial amount of an associate. [IAS 28 paras 10, 32].
	The carrying amount of the investment is adjusted by the investor's share of the results of its investee less any amortisation or write-off of goodwill, the investor's share of any relevant gains or losses, and any other changes in the investee's net assets.	The carrying amount is adjusted to reflect the investor's share of the profit or loss, other comprehensive income and equity of the associate, as well as any impairment. [FRS 102 para 14.8].	IAS 28 is not clear in this matter. The definition of 'equity accounting' in the standard requires changes in the net assets to be recognised by the investor, but elsewhere the standard refers to changes in profit or loss and other comprehensive income. [IAS 28 para 10].
	The investor's share of its associate's operating results is included immediately after group operating profit. The investor's share of any non-operating exceptional items, interest and tax is shown separately from the amounts for the group.	The investor's share of the associate's profit or loss and other comprehensive income are presented in the statement of comprehensive income. Distributions received from the associate reduce the carrying amount of the investment. [FRS 102 paras 14.8(a), 14.14].	Same as new UK GAAP. [IAS 28 para 10].

	Old UK GAAP	New UK GAAP (FRS 102)	IFRS
	Under FRS 9, losses continue to be equity accounted. The investor continues to use the equity method, even if this results in an interest in net liabilities.	In a situation of losses in excess of the investment, after the investor's interest is reduced to zero, additional losses are provided for to the extent that the investor has incurred legal or constructive obligations or has made payments on behalf of the associate. [FRS 102 para 14.8(h)].	Same as new UK GAAP. [IAS 28 paras 38-39].
	The investor's share of any profits or losses from transactions between the investor and its investee, that are included in the carrying amount of assets in either entity, are eliminated in the investor's consolidated financial statements. [FRS 9 paras 4, 27, 36, 44].	Unrealised losses and profits resulting from transactions with associates are eliminated to the extent of the investor's interest in the associate. [FRS 102 para 14.8(e)].	Same as new UK GAAP. IAS 28 paras 28-29].
	Where there has been an impairment to any goodwill attributable to an associate, this is written down. Any impairment in the underlying net assets of an associate are normally reflected within the associate itself, and so no further provision by the investor should usually be necessary. [FRS 9 para 38].	If there is an indication that an investment in an associate is impaired, the entire carrying amount is tested for impairment as a single asset. Any goodwill included as part of the carrying amount is not tested separately. [FRS 102 para 14.8(d)].	Same as new UK GAAP. IAS 39 is used for indicators of impairment, which are then measured in accordance with IAS 36. [IAS 28 para 40].
	When an entity ceases to be an associate, the initial carrying amount of any retained interest is based on the final carrying amount for the former associate at the date the entity ceased to qualify as such (written down, if necessary, to its recoverable amount). [FRS 9 para 42].	An investor discontinues the use of the equity method when it ceases to have significant influence. Where an associate is disposed of, the gain/loss is the difference between the proceeds less the carrying amount relating to the proportion disposed of. In addition, the gain or loss includes amounts recognised in other comprehensive income in relation to the associate that are required to be reclassified to profit or loss on disposal under other sections of FRS 102. Under new UK GAAP, a part of an associate can be disposed of. The retained investment's carrying amount at the date when it ceases to be an associate is regarded as its cost on initial measurement as a financial asset. [FRS 102 para 14.8(i)].	Different from new UK GAAP. When an entity ceases to be an associate, any investment is remeasured to fair value at that date and is recognised as a financial asset in accordance with IAS 39. [IAS 28 para 22(b)].

	Old UK GAAP	New UK GAAP (FRS 102)	IFRS
Classification and presentation	The investor's share of the net assets of its associates is shown as a separate item in fixed asset investments. [FRS 9 para 29].	Similar to old UK GAAP. An investor normally classifies investments in associates as fixed assets. Associates are presented as a separate line item on the balance sheet. [FRS 102 para 14.11].	Similar to old UK GAAP and new UK GAAP; however, only those associates accounted for using the equity method are presented as a separate non-current line item. [IAS 1 para 54(e); IAS 28 para 15].
Separate or individual financial statements	In the investor's separate financial statements, its interests in associates should be treated as fixed asset investments and shown either at cost less any amounts written off, or at valuation. Changes in valuation are recognised in the statement of total recognised gains and losses. [FRS 9 para 26].	Where an investor that is a parent prepares separate financial statements, it adopts a policy of accounting for all of its associates either: • at cost less impairment; • at fair value through profit or loss; or • at fair value through other comprehensive income. [FRS 102 para 9.26].	Where an investor that is a parent prepares separate financial statements, it accounts for investments in associates either: • at cost; or • in accordance with IAS 39; or • In accordance with the equity method for period started on or after 1 January 2016 (early adoption is permitted). Also, investments are accounted for in accordance with IFRS 5 where they are classified as held for sale. [IAS 27 para 10].
		An investor that is not a parent can account for its associates in its individual financial statements using: • cost less impairment; • fair value model with revaluation through other comprehensive income; or • fair value through profit or loss. [FRS 102 para 14.4].	Differs from new UK GAAP. An investor that is not a parent accounts for its associates using the equity method, unless it is exempt. [IAS 28 para 16]. These are often referred to as 'economic interest' financial statements.
Cost model	Not permitted, except in the investor's separate financial statements or if the 'investment fund' exemption applies. [FRS 9 paras 26, 49].	An investor that is not a parent can elect to measure associates under the cost model. [FRS 102 para 14.4].	Not permitted, except in separate financial statements. [IAS 28 para 44].
Fair value model	Not permitted, except in the investor's separate financial statements or if the 'investment fund' exemption applies. For fair value accounting, the alternative accounting rules under company law are adopted. Changes in fair value are recognised in the statement of total recognised gains and losses. [FRS 9 para 26].	In its individual financial statements, an investor that is not a parent might elect to measure investments in associates under the fair value model (that is, fair value with revaluation through other comprehensive income) or at fair value through profit or loss. [FRS 102 paras 14.4, 14.9, 14.10]. Entities that prepare consolidated financial statements because they are a parent should	Venture capital organisations, mutual funds, unit trusts and similar entities can designate associates as at fair value through profit or loss. [IAS 28 para 19]. Fair value through profit or loss is also permitted in separate financial statements if IAS 39 is used. [IAS 28 para 44].

	Old UK GAAP	New UK GAAP (FRS 102)	IFRS
		measure investments in associates at fair value through profit or loss where these are held as part of an investment portfolio. [FRS 102 para 14.4B].	

Investments in joint ventures

	Old UK GAAP	New UK GAAP (FRS 102)	IFRS
Definition	A joint venture is an entity in which the reporting entity holds an interest on a long-term basis and that is jointly controlled by the reporting entity and one or more venturers under a contractual agreement. [FRS 9 para 4].	A joint venture is a contractual arrangement in which two or more parties (the venturers) undertake an economic activity that is subject to joint control. Joint control is the contractually agreed sharing of control over an economic activity; it exists only where the strategic financial and operating decisions relating to the activity require the unanimous consent of the parties sharing the control. [FRS 102 para 15.2].	Same as new UK GAAP. [IFRS 11 para 4]. IFRS 11 includes guidance on contractual arrangements.
Types of joint venture	FRS 9 distinguishes between: • a jointly controlled entity; and • a joint arrangement that is not an entity. [FRS 9 paras 8, 10].	Similar to old UK GAAP, but there are three categories of joint venture: • jointly controlled entities, in which the arrangement is carried on through a separate entity (company or partnership); • jointly controlled operations, in which each venturer uses its own assets for a specific project; and • jointly controlled assets, which is a project carried on with assets that are jointly controlled (and often jointly owned). [FRS 102 paras 15.3 –15.8].	IFRS 11 classifies joint arrangements into two types: • joint operations, which give parties to the arrangement direct rights to the assets and obligations for the liabilities; and • joint ventures, which give the parties rights to the net assets or outcome of the arrangement. [IFRS 11 paras 14 –16].
Accounting for jointly controlled entities	FRS 9 requires use of the gross equity method in consolidated financial statements and does not permit use of proportionate consolidation. The gross equity method is similar to the equity method used in accounting for investments in associates, but with additional disclosures. [FRS 9 para 20]. However, certain investment funds are permitted to include all investments in their investment portfolio (including those over which they have	In its consolidated financial statements, a venturer accounts for a jointly controlled entity by using the equity method of accounting. If a jointly controlled entity is held as part of an investment portfolio, it is measured at fair value with changes recognised in profit or loss. [FRS 102 paras 15.9A, 15.9B].	Under IFRS 11, a joint venturer must account for its interest in a joint venture using the equity method in accordance with IAS 28. [IFRS 11 para 24], unless the venture qualifies for the fair value model (see below).

	Old UK GAAP	New UK GAAP (FRS 102)	IFRS
	joint control), either at cost or at market value. [FRS 9 para 49].		
Gross equity method/equity method	The gross equity method is an expansion of the equity method (see 'accounting for associates'). The investor's share of the aggregate gross assets and liabilities underlying the net amount included for the investment is shown on the balance sheet; the investor's share of the investee's turnover is shown in the profit and loss accounts, in addition to the items shown under the equity method. [FRS 9 paras 4-21].	See 'investments in associates' above. [FRS 102 para 15.13].	Similar to new UK GAAP. [IAS 28 paras 10, 32; IFRS 11 para 24].
Proportionate consolidation	Not permitted.	Not permitted.	Under IFRS 11, proportional consolidation is not allowed.
Accounting for contributions to/ transactions with a jointly controlled entity	The investor's share of any profits or losses from transactions between the investor and its investee, that are included in the carrying amount of assets in either entity, are eliminated in the investor's consolidated financial statements. [FRS 9 para 36]. UITF 31 provides guidance on exchange of businesses or other non-monetary assets for an interest in a subsidiary, joint venture or associate.	Similar to old UK GAAP. Gains and losses on contribution or sales of assets to a joint venture by a venturer are recognised to the same extent as that of the interests of the other venturers, provided the assets are retained by the joint venture, and significant risks and rewards of ownership of the contributed assets have been transferred. The venturer recognises the full amount of any loss where there is evidence of impairment loss from the contribution or sale. [FRS 102 paras 15.16, 15.17].	Same as new UK GAAP. [IFRS 11 paras B34–B37].
Accounting for a joint arrangement that is not an entity/jointly controlled operations	Participants in a joint arrangement that is not an entity should account for their own assets, liabilities and cash flows according to the terms of the agreement governing the arrangement. [FRS 9 para 18].	Similar to old UK GAAP. A venturer in a joint operation recognises in its financial statements: • the assets that it controls; • the liabilities that it incurs; • the expenses that it incurs; and • its share of income from the sale of goods or services by the joint venture. [FRS 102 para 15.5].	Same as new UK GAAP. [IFRS 11 para 20].
Accounting for jointly controlled assets	See 'accounting for a joint arrangement that is not an entity' above.	A venturer accounts for its share of the jointly controlled assets, liabilities, income and expenses, and any liabilities and expenses that it has incurred. [FRS 102 para 15.7].	Same as new UK GAAP. [IFRS 11 para 20].

	Old UK GAAP	New UK GAAP (FRS 102)	IFRS
Separate and individual financial statements	Investments in joint ventures should be treated as fixed asset investments in the investor's separate financial statements. They are shown either at cost, less any amount written off, or at valuation. If the valuation method is adopted, changes in the valuation are recognised in the statement of total recognised gains and losses. [FRS 9 para 20].	Where a venturer that is a parent prepares separate financial statements, it adopts a policy of accounting for all of its jointly controlled entities either: • at cost less impairment; • at fair value through profit and loss; or • at fair value through other comprehensive income. [FRS 102 para 9.26].	Where an investor that is a parent prepares separate financial statements, it accounts for investments in jointly controlled entities either: • at cost; or • in accordance with IAS 39. Also, investments are accounted for in accordance with IFRS 5 where they are classified as held for sale. [IFRS 11 paras 26-27].
		A venturer that is not a parent can account for its jointly controlled entities in its individual financial statements using: • cost less impairment; or • the fair value model with revaluation through other comprehensive income; or • fair value through profit or loss. [FRS 102 para 15.9].	Differs from new UK GAAP. A venturer that is not a parent accounts for its jointly controlled entities using the equity method, unless it is exempt. [IFRS 11 para 24]. These are often referred to as 'economic interest' financial statements.
Cost model	Not permitted, except in the investor's separate financial statements or if the 'investment fund' exemption applies. [FRS 9 para 48].	A venturer that is not a parent can elect to measure jointly controlled entities under the cost model. [FRS 102 para 15.10].	Not permitted, except, in separate financial statements. [IFRS 11 para 26].
Fair value model	Not permitted, except in the investor's separate financial statements or if the 'investment fund' exemption applies. For fair value accounting, the alternative accounting rules under company law are adopted. Changes in fair value are recognised in the statement of total recognised gains and losses. [FRS 9 para 20].	In its individual financial statements, a venturer that is not a parent might elect to measure jointly controlled entities under the fair value model (that is, fair value with revaluation through other comprehensive income) or at fair value through profit or loss. [FRS 102 paras 15.9, 15.14]. Entities who prepare consolidated financial statements because they are a parent should measure jointly controlled entities at fair value through profit or loss where these are held as part of an investment portfolio. [FRS 102 para 15.9B].	Venture capital organisations, mutual funds, unit trusts and similar entities can designate joint ventures as at fair value through profit or loss on initial recognition. [IAS 28 para 18].

5. Other subjects

Related party disclosures

	Old UK GAAP	New UK GAAP (FRS 102)	IFRS
Definitions			
Definition	A related party is a person or entity that is related to the entity that is preparing its financial statements (the reporting entity). A person (or a close member of that person's family) is a related party if that person has control, joint control or significant influence over the reporting entity, or is a member of the key management personnel of the reporting entity or its parent. An entity is a related party if: • it is a member of the same group as the reporting entity; • one entity is an associate or joint venture of the other entity; • both entities are joint ventures of the same third party; • one entity is a joint venture and the other is an associate of the same third entity; • the entity is a retirement benefit scheme for employees of the reporting entity (or an entity related to it); if the entity is itself such a scheme, the sponsoring employer is a related party of that scheme; • the entity is controlled or jointly controlled by a related person (see above); or • a person having control or joint control over the reporting entity has significant influence over the entity or is a member of its key management personnel (or of its parent). [FRS 8 para 2.5].	Same as old UK GAAP, but with an additional related party added in the July 2015 amendments to FRS 102. An entity is related to a reporting entity if the entity (or any member of a group of which it is a part) provides key management personnel services to the reporting entity or to the parent of the reporting entity. [FRS 102 para 33.2].	Same as the updated new UK GAAP. [IAS 24 para 9].

	Old UK GAAP	New UK GAAP (FRS 102)	IFRS
Disclosures	If there have been material related party transactions, the following are disclosed: • names of the transacting related parties; • a description of the related party relationship; • a description of the transactions; • the amounts involved; • any other elements necessary for an understanding of the financial statements; • the amounts due to and from related parties at the balance sheet date; and • the amounts written off. [FRS 8 para 6]. Commitments are not specifically referred to as a disclosure requirement, but they may fall to be disclosed as an element necessary for an understanding of the financial statements.	Where there have been related party transactions, disclosure is made of the nature of the relationship, as well as information about the transactions, outstanding balances and commitments necessary for an understanding of the financial statements. As a minimum, disclosures include: • the amount of the transactions; • outstanding balances (including their terms and conditions, whether they are secured, and details of any guarantees); • provisions for uncollectible receivables; and the expense recognised for bad debts. [FRS 102 para 33.9].	Same as new UK GAAP. [IAS 24 para 18].
	Disclosures may be aggregated for similar transactions by type of related party. [FRS 8 para 21].	Disclosure is made separately for each of the following categories: • entities with control, joint control or significant influence over the entity; • entities over which the entity has control, joint control or significant influence; • key management personnel of the entity and its parent; • entities that provide key management personnel services to the entity (added in the July 2015 amendments); and • other related parties. [FRS 102 para 33.10].	IFRS requires a more detailed breakdown of the categories than new UK GAAP. [IAS 24 paras 18A, 19]. *FRS 101 RDF (IFRS): Qualifying entities are exempt from the requirement in para 18A of IAS 24 to disclose the cost of key management personnel services provided by an entity (under the July 2015 amendments to FRS 101). [FRS 101 para 8(j)].*
	Disclosure is not required of the relationship and transactions between the reporting entity and any other party where the relationship arises simply from that party's role as finance provider, utility company or government departments and agencies. [FRS 8 para 4].	Same as old UK GAAP. [FRS 102 para 33.4(c)].	Same as new UK GAAP. [IAS 24 para 11(c)].

	Old UK GAAP	New UK GAAP (FRS 102)	IFRS
	There is no disclosure exemption for state-controlled entities.	There is an exemption from the disclosure requirements where: • the state has control, joint control or significant influence over the entity, or • another entity is a related party because it is controlled, jointly controlled or under the significant influence of the same state as the reporting entity. Entities taking this exemption must still disclose any parent-subsidiary relationship. [FRS 102 para 33.11].	There is an exemption for state-controlled entities for accounting periods beginning on or after 1 January 2011. Paragraph 26 of IAS 24 requires some high-level disclosures if the exemption is taken.
	Transactions between members of a group are exempt from disclosures, provided that any subsidiary undertaking that is a party to the transaction is a wholly owned member of the group. [FRS 8 para 3(c)].	Same as old UK GAAP. [FRS 102 para 33.1A].	Under IFRS, there are no exemptions for members of a group. *FRS 101 RDF (IFRS): Same as new UK GAAP. There is an exemption from disclosing related party transactions entered into between members of a group, provided that any subsidiary that is a party to the transaction is a wholly owned member of the group. [FRS 101 para 8(k)].*
Key management personnel	Disclosures of key management personnel compensation are not required by FRS 8. [FRS 8 para 3(e)]. However, there are disclosure requirements for directors' remuneration in company law. These apply regardless of the GAAP applied.	An entity discloses key management personnel compensation in total. [FRS 102 para 33.7].	Similar to new UK GAAP, with additional breakdown into five categories of compensation. [IAS 24 para 17]. *FRS 101 RDF (IFRS): Qualifying entities are exempt from this IAS 24 disclosure. [FRS 101 para 8(j)].*
Other	Irrespective of the existence of transactions, an entity discloses: • the name and relationship of the controlling party; and • the name of the ultimate controlling party, if different. [FRS 8 para 5].	An entity discloses the name of its parent and, if different, the ultimate controlling party. [FRS 102 para 33.5].	Same as new UK GAAP. [IAS 24 para 13].

Specialised activities

	Old UK GAAP	New UK GAAP (FRS 102)	IFRS
Agriculture			
Definitions	There is no definition of biological or agricultural assets.	• Biological asset: a living animal or plant. • Agricultural produce: the harvested product of biological assets. [FRS 102 Glossary].	Same as new UK GAAP. [IFRS Glossary].
Recognition and measurement	There is no discrete guidance in UK GAAP on accounting for biological assets. In practice, such assets are accounted for as tangible fixed assets or stock.	For each class of biological asset and its related agricultural produce, an entity can choose as its accounting policy either: • the fair value model; or • the cost model. [FRS 102 para 34.3A].	IFRS requires an entity to use the fair value model. Exemption from measurement at fair value is only allowed if the fair value cannot be measured reliably. This is the case for biological assets for which market-determined prices or values are not available, and for which alternative estimates of fair value are determined to be clearly unreliable. In such cases, biological assets are measured at cost. [IAS 41 paras 12-13, 30].
Fair value model	Not applicable.	If an entity adopts the fair value model, the following accounting applies. Biological assets are measured on initial recognition and at each reporting date at fair value less costs to sell. Changes in fair value less costs to sell are recognised in profit or loss. [FRS 102 para 34.4]. Agricultural produce is measured at the point of harvest at fair value less costs to sell. [FRS 102 para 34.5].	Same as new UK GAAP. [IAS 41 paras 12, 13, 26].
Cost model	No specific guidance for agricultural assets.	If an entity adopts the cost model, the following accounting applies. Biological assets are measured at cost less any accumulated depreciation and any accumulated impairment losses. [FRS 102 para 34.8]. Agricultural produce is measured at the point of harvest at either:	Same as new UK GAAP for biological assets. [IAS 41 para 30]. Similar to new UK GAAP for agricultural produce, but IFRS does not include a choice of measuring this at cost; it has to be measured at fair value less estimated costs to sell at the point of harvest. [IAS 41 para 32].

	Old UK GAAP	New UK GAAP (FRS 102)	IFRS
		• the lower of cost and estimated selling price less costs to complete and sell; or • its fair value less costs to sell. Any gain or loss arising on initial recognition of agricultural produce at fair value less costs to sell is included in profit or loss for the period in which it arises. [FRS 102 para 34.9].	
Bearer plants	No specific guidance for bearer plants.	Bearer plants are not scoped out from section 34 of FRS 102 on agriculture and, therefore, are accounted for in the same way as other biological assets.	An amendment to IAS 16 and IAS 41 effective for annual periods beginning on or after 1 January 2016 defines bearer plants as "*a living plant that:* *(a) is used in the production or supply of agricultural produce;* *(b) is expected to bear produce for more than one period; and* *(c) has a remote likelihood of being sold as agricultural produce, except for incidental scrap sales.*" Bearer plants represent items of property, plant and equipment under IFRS and are accounted for in accordance with IAS 16. The produce on bearer plants is still accounted for as agricultural produce under IAS 41.
Extractive industries			
Recognition and measurement	There is no discrete guidance on accounting for extractive industries.	An entity that is engaged in the exploration for and/or evaluation of mineral resources (extractive activities) applies the requirements of IFRS 6. References made to other IFRSs within IFRS 6 are taken to be references to the relevant section or paragraph within FRS 102. [FRS 102 paras 34.11, 34.11A].	Exploration and evaluation assets are measured at cost. An entity may develop a policy to determine which expenditures are recognised as exploration and evaluation assets. IFRS restricts recognition of certain types of expenditure as an asset. [IFRS 6 paras 8-9].
Service concession arrangements			
Definition	FRS 5 Application Note F provides guidance on accounting for 'private finance initiative and similar contracts'.	A service concession arrangement is an arrangement whereby a government or other public sector body contracts with a private operator to develop, operate and maintain infrastructure assets such as roads, prisons and hospitals. [FRS 102 para 34.12].	Same as new UK GAAP. [IFRIC 12 para 2].

	Old UK GAAP	New UK GAAP (FRS 102)	IFRS
Accounting – operator	Where it is concluded that the operator does not have a physical asset, it will instead recognise a financial asset representing the debt due from the purchaser/ grantor for the fair value of the property. This is reduced as payments are received. In addition, finance income is recognised using an asset-specific rate. Where it is concluded that the physical asset should be recognised by the operator, it will be capitalised as a fixed asset under the rules in FRS 15. If the operator's fixed asset is transferred back to the purchaser/ grantor for a fixed amount on expiry, it is depreciated over the shorter of the project term and its useful life to that fixed amount (which can be nil). [FRS 5 App Note F].	The operator recognises a financial asset or an intangible asset. A financial asset is recognised to the extent that the operator has an unconditional contractual right to receive cash or another financial asset from, or at the direction of, the grantor for the construction services. An intangible asset is recognised to the extent that the operator receives a right (or licence) to charge users of the public service. The financial and intangible assets are initially measured at fair value. They are subsequently measured in accordance with section 11, 12 and/or 18 of FRS 102, as applicable. [FRS 102 paras 34.13-34.15]. Borrowing costs attributable to the arrangement are recognised as an expense, unless the operator has an intangible asset, in which case borrowing costs may be capitalised during the construction phase where a policy of capitalisation has been adopted in accordance with section 25. [FRS 102 para 34.16A].	Similar to new UK GAAP, but guidance is more detailed. [IFRIC 12 paras 15-17, 22, 23, 26].
Accounting – grantor/ purchaser	Where it is concluded that the purchaser/ grantor has an asset of the property and a liability, these are recorded in its balance sheet. The initial amount recorded for each is the fair value of the property. Where it is concluded that the purchaser/ grantor does not have an asset of the property, the purchaser records payments as an expense as they are incurred. [FRS 5 App Note F].	The grantor recognises its interest in the infrastructure asset usually as property, plant and equipment or as intangible assets, as appropriate, with a corresponding liability measured using a finance lease model. [FRS 102 paras 34.12E-34.12H]. Where, as a result of applying finance lease requirements (section 20 of FRS 102), the grantor has not recognised a liability to make payments to the operator, it does not recognise the infrastructure assets. [FRS 102 para 34.12F].	IFRIC 12 does not cover accounting by grantors; it only covers accounting by operators. [IFRIC 12 para 9].

	Old UK GAAP	New UK GAAP (FRS 102)	IFRS
Other			

		FRS 102 also includes the following sections:
		• Financial institutions.
		• Retirement benefit plans.
		• Heritage assets.
		• Funding commitments.
		• Public benefit entities:
		  • Incoming resources from non-exchange transactions.
		  • Public benefit entity combinations.
		  • Concessionary loans.